Fish

Fish

Jean-Paul Grappe

Photography Pierre Beauchemin

Fitzhenry & Whiteside

Fish © 2011 Fitzhenry & Whiteside Ltd.
Originally published in French, copyright © 2006 by Les Éditions de l'Homme
955, rue Amherst, Montréal (Québec) H2L 3K4, Canada
Translation copyright © 2011 by Fitzhenry & Whiteside Ltd.
195 Allstate Parkway, Markham, Ontario L3R 4T8
Published in the United States by Fitzhenry & Whiteside,
311 Washington Street, Brighton, Massachusetts 02135

www.fitzhenry.ca   godwit@fitzhenry.ca

Fitzhenry & Whiteside acknowledges with thanks the Canada Council for the Arts, and the
Ontario Arts Council for their support of our publishing program. We acknowledge the
financial support of the Government of Canada through the Book Publishing Industry
Development Program (BPIDP) for our publishing activities.

Canada Council   Conseil des Arts   ONTARIO ARTS COUNCIL
for the Arts   du Canada   CONSEIL DES ARTS DE L'ONTARIO

Library and Archives Canada Cataloguing
in Publication
Grappe, Jean-Paul
Fish / Jean-Paul Grappe ;
photographer, Pierre Beauchemin.
Includes index.
Translation of: Poissons.
ISBN 978-1-55455-203-0
1. Cookery (Fish).   I. Title.
TX747.G7213 2011   641.6'92
C2011-903768-5

Publisher Cataloging-in-Publication Data (U.S)

Grappe, Jean-Paul.
Fish / Jean-Paul Grappe.
[144] p. : col. photos. ;   cm.
Includes index.
ISBN: 978-1-55455-203-0   (pbk.)
1. Cooking (Fish).   I. Title.
641.692 dc22   TX747.G7377 2011

Photos: Pierre Beauchemin
Culinary stylist: Jacques Faucher
Accessories stylist: Luce Meunier
Kitchen accessories: Arthur Quentin (Montreal)
Translated by Janet and Chris Guillard
Printed and bound in Hong Kong, China

10 9 8 7 6 5 4 3 2 1

Contents

The Team from left to right:
Luce Meunier, staging stylist;
Jean-Paul Grappe;
Myriam Pelletier, culinary stylist;
Pierre Beauchemin, culinary photographer;
Julie Léger (behind the camera), photographer.

EATING FISH

Today, we have rediscovered the value of fish, even though we still have some reservations about fish in general and some fish products in particular—despite the fact that fish should be considered as "noble" a food as lobster, crab, or shrimp. Moreover, fine cooking has always given a privileged place to the products of the sea in its gastronomic menus. All cookbooks, old or new, give as many descriptions of, and preparations for, products of the sea as they do to "earth" foods. A number of great chefs have even seen their skills honed by preparing dishes entirely devoted to fish and seafood.

Unfortunately, most people have little knowledge of fish. We only know the names of a few species but not their shape or color. We are also hesitant about cooking them, for various reasons, but mostly because we lack information about how to prepare fish.

In the past, you found only frozen fish in markets. More recently, some pioneers—specialty fish stores and a small number of restaurant owners ahead of their time—have again begun to value fish and to inspire consumers to enjoy it. To their credit, these restaurant owners are choosing fresh fish. Faster modern transportation makes it easier to get a supply of fresh products all year round. Fish arrives at its destination within 24 to 36 hours from its arrival at the wharf; however, large cities are often located far from the source, which makes supplying fresh fish difficult. Therefore it's important to be vigilant when choosing fish and to check for products that may

have been frozen. You should be careful not to buy previously frozen fish, believing it to be fresh.

Since nutrition has become a major pre-occupation for people who care about their health, and since dieticians and nutritionists are making known the nutritional value of fish, it has regained its rightful place in the food chain. Like meat and poultry, fish contains a lot of protein. It can easily replace beef, pork, or chicken and be served several times a week.

Some people have the impression that fish is less nutritious than meat. Actually, fish is easier to digest as it contains only 5% connective tissue compared to 14% in meat. Moreover, fish does not contain fiber, which is sometimes difficult to digest. Lab tests have shown that 90% of fish protein is digestible.

For people who watch their weight, fish has the advantage of delivering far fewer calories than meat. Of course this is true only if the fish is prepared in a simple way: in a court-bouillon, steamed, or grilled. We don't recommend fried fish for people who are on a low-calorie diet. It is also advisable for these people to select their fish carefully, since fish is divided into two categories: lean and fat.

BUYING GUIDE FOR FRESH FISH

In choosing fresh fish, it is important to check for certain indicators of freshness.

Odor: Most salt water fish have a light smell of seaweed, except for ray-finned fish, which sometimes have a slight odor of ammonia. Fresh water fish have an odor of aquatic herbs.

Body: A fresh fish should be firm, with a shiny appearance.

Eye: Fish eyes must be clear, bright, and convex, filling the entire cavity of the eye socket.

Skin: The skin of fresh fish is tight and adheres well to the bones.

Scales: When fresh, fish are covered with bright scales firmly attached to the skin.

Gills: The gills of fresh fish must be bright, moist, and be pink or blood-red in color. However, the gills of some salt water fish, like sole, have less accentuated color. The gills can be blackish, brown, or dark in color.

Flesh: When pressed with a finger, the flesh of a fresh fish must be firm and elastic. It can be white, pink, or red, as with some species of tuna. When cut, the flesh of large salt water fish has a satin appearance.

BUYING GUIDE FOR FROZEN FISH

When purchasing frozen fish, it is important to be vigilant and to buy fish that has preferably been vacuum-packed and identified as a "frozen product." Ideally, the date of freezing should be shown on the label, which will help in assessing how long a frozen fish can be kept (see Table on page 11). Some fish may have been poorly frozen and others may have been re-frozen. It is therefore important to carefully check the appearance of frozen fish. There should not be any brownish color showing or dried spots on the thinner parts.

STORING FRESH FISH

Once you are satisfied that the fish was fresh when you bought it, it is important to keep it that way. Of course, you can't keep it for more than four or five days, even if it has been packaged in the best conditions, between 0°C and 4°C (32°F to 39°F). Short of having a refrigerator specifically designed with a fish drawer, you will have to make your own fish rack. This method consists of setting a cloth-covered rack in a plastic container, laying the fresh fish on it, and covering it with another cloth, then placing the container on crushed ice or ice cubes. The fish should not be in contact with the ice, as it could get freezer "burn." Moreover, the fish should not soak in the water from the thawing ice. The water must be emptied regularly and ice added as required to maintain the ideal temperature.

STORING FROZEN FISH

All fish purchased in a frozen state must be kept at a temperature of -18°C (-4°F) to stop any bacterial activity. However, it is preferable not to keep frozen fish too long as the flesh dries, becomes tough, and gets freezer burn. It is best to "frost up" the fish by soaking it in water to protect it from dehydration and oxidation.

FREEZING AND FLASH FREEZING

The main objective is to transform a maximum amount of water into ice and thus considerably extend the length of time frozen food can be stored. These methods can apply just as well to fresh produce. It is important that these two techniques be appropriately applied when freezing or flash freezing and maintaining the required temperatures during storage.

While regular freezing is a method that takes a period of time, flash freezing is much faster. The latter technique has many advantages. Flash freezing consists of freezing a product at a very low temperature, -40°C (-40°F), so that it freezes very quickly below the temperature range of -1°C to -15°C (30°F to 5°F), called the crystallization zone. This zone is the most important in the freezing and flash freezing processes because it is at this point that the water contained in the fish (80% to 90%) changes to ice crystals.

When freezing takes place slowly, the crystals are large, while a faster freezing produces smaller crystals. The large crystals have a greater tendency to alter products than small crystals. Also, the large crystals create a larger liquid build up. This will result in a drier meat or fish. A fish that has been properly flash frozen will keep its fresh qualities better than a fresh fish poorly conserved or a fish that has been frozen. It's important to note that fish should be flash-frozen very soon after coming out of the water.

Ideally, it is best to flash-freeze a fish if you want to keep it for a long time. However, if you don't have flash-freezing equipment, simple freezing is adequate.

Both techniques require some precautions to achieve a quality product.

It is important to adhere to the following procedures:

- Always wash, gut, and scale the fish
- Choose a good packing material before freezing or flash-freezing fish
- Ideally, choose vacuum packing
- Short of this, use a plastic wrap rather than aluminum or any other wrapping material to minimize the amount of air around the fish
- Do not forget to label the fish with the freezing date
- Do not re-freeze a thawed fish

METHOD AND COOKING TIMES

There are basic rules and precise methods for cooking fish. Generally, the methods for cooking meat can also be applied to fish. However, fish should not be cooked too long, as you run the risk of it becoming dry. The flesh will toughen and lose its flavor. Fish can be prepared in many different ways and can be used in various dishes like soups, pâtés, mousses, or fish loaf. A number of cooking methods can be applied to fish.

VARIOUS COOKING METHODS

English cooking: This method consists of cooking the fish in butter, in a pan, after having coated it in flour, dipped it in a mixture of beaten egg and milk, and then covered it in bread crumbs.

Cooking "à la meunière": This method of cooking is mainly used with small fish. Dip the fish in flour, then sauté them in a pan with butter.

Steam cooking: This is when you cook the fish by steaming it with a court-bouillon of white wine or fish stock, by using a steamer or a rack set in a pan, covered with a lid. There are many commercial steamers on the market that can be used.

Cooking "bain-marie": This culinary method is used for fish mousse and fish loaf. The dish containing the preparation to be cooked is first placed in a double boiler that can then be put on the stove element or in the oven.

Baking: Large pieces of fish can be baked in the oven with butter and vegetables. It is important to baste often with cooking juices.

Baking "en papillote": Fish cooked "en papillote" are wrapped in buttered aluminum foil or parchment paper, along with finely diced vegetables and a little white wine or fish stock. The papillote is then placed in the oven to bake as it braises in its own juices.

Deep frying: Before deep frying a fish, it is necessary to coat it with batter or simply roll it in flour, then gently drop it into a pot of boiling oil.

Poaching (braising): This method is used mostly for large pieces of fish, and consists of cooking the fish in a small amount of liquid (white wine or fish stock) with finely diced vegetables. It is preferable to use the oven for this method.

Court-bouillon poaching: The fish cooks in a court-bouillon, containing white wine, fish stock or water, carrots, onions, bouquet garni, freshly squeezed lemon juice, salt, and pepper.

COOKING FISH WITH HERBS

In these recipes, we always suggest using fresh herbs, which can now be found all year round. The given amounts are therefore for fresh herbs. If you cannot get fresh herbs, dried herbs can be used but in much smaller quantity.

COOKING TIME

While cooking, the protein in fish (albumin) tends to coagulate. The fish is cooked when this substance (white liquid) comes slightly out of the fish. The cooking time varies from 9 to 11 minutes for a fresh fish 2.5 cm (1") thick, and from 12 to 22 minutes for a frozen fish. Cooking times vary according to the type and quality of the fish. Also, a lean fish can cook faster than one containing more fat.

NOTE: It is important to note that the cooking times given in the recipes are always subject to thickness, quality, freshness, and type of fish used.

Using a Thermometer in Modern Cooking

When I first learned my trade, 50 years ago, our chef taught us cooking "by touch." Today it is imperative to use a thermometer to cook food to precise temperatures. It's important to understand that fish never have the same thickness, and the times given are always approximate. All the recipes in this book are based on reaching a temperature of 68°C (155°F) in the center of the fish. However, Dr. Pierre Gélinas in his book *Répertoire des microorganismes pathogènes*, tells us that we can cook fish to 80°C (180°F) **and reach 52°C (125°F) in the center** of the fish without any problem. It is up to us to decide, based on the quality of the fish and the temperature at which it should be cooked.

	Fresh Fish		Frozen Fish			
	0°C to 4°C 32°F to 40°F	Fresh 4°C to 10°C 40°F to 50°F	Fresh Frozen 0°C to 40°C 32°F to 104°F	Flash Frozen -10°C to -18°C 14°F to -4°F	Flash Frozen -18°C to -25°C -4°F to -13°F	Flash Frozen -30°C -22°F
Storage Time for Fatty Fish	4 to 10 days	none	2 months	4 months	8 months	12 months
Storage Time for lean Fish	4 to 10 days	none	1 ½ months	8 months	18 months	24 months
Storage Time for Flat Fish	4 to 10 days	none	4 months	10 months	24 months	23 months
Development of Pathogenic Bacteria[1]	Slow	Rapid	Stop	Stop	Stop	Stop
Development of Deterioration of Bacteria[2]	Fairly Slow	Very Fast	Very Slow	Stop	Stop	Stop
Chemical Reactions: Tanning and Rancidity[3]	–	–	Fairly Fast	Slow	Very Slow	Very Slow

NOTES: STORAGE TIME FOR FRESH AND FROZEN FISH

1. Pathogenic bacteria: This bacteria produces toxins that may lead to food poisoning.
2. Deterioration bacteria: These produce waste that alters the taste, smell, and appearance of the food and reduces their storage time.
3. Chemical reactions such as brown spots and rancidity can be caused by poor methods of freezing, flash-freezing, or poor packaging. The fish may show a brownish color on its thinner parts.

The Basics of Successful Fish Recipes

FISH STOCK

22 ml (1 1/2 tbsp) butter
800 g (1 3/4 lbs) fish bones and trimmings (preferably flat fish)
75 g (3/4 cup) onions, finely sliced
125 g (1 1/4 cups) leeks, finely sliced
125 g (1 1/4 cups) celery, finely sliced
90 ml (6 tbsp) shallots, finely sliced
150 g (2 1/2 cups) mushrooms, finely sliced
125 ml (1/2 cup) dry white wine
20 ml (4 tsp) fresh lemon juice
1 litre (4 cups) cold water
1 pinch thyme
1/2 bay leaf
10 peppercorns

• In a saucepan, heat the butter. Sweat (cook on low) the fish bones and trimmings and all the vegetables for 4 to 5 minutes. Add the wine, lemon juice, cold water; add the thyme, bay leaf, and peppercorns. Bring to the boil and then simmer 25 minutes. Pour all ingredients into a conical sieve and reserve the fish stock for future use.

NOTE: The stock may be frozen for 3 to 4 months. Do not use carrots in the preparation of a fish stock as this gives a sweet flavor to the bouillon. Never add salt to a stock as some recipes call for it to be reduced to a concentrated form.

COURT-BOUILLON

A court-bouillon is not often used. However, it is a high quality aromatic base for poaching fish (small or large pieces).

2.5 litres (10 cups) water
125 ml (1/2 cup) white wine
125 ml (1/2 cup) good quality white wine vinegar
30 ml (2 tbsp) coarse salt
300 g (2 cups) onions, finely sliced
300 g (2 2/3 cups) carrots, finely sliced
1 bouquet garni
10 peppercorns

• In a saucepan, place all the ingredients and cook until the carrots and onions are tender. If the court-bouillon is used immediately, reserve the carrots as a garnish for fish or shellfish and strain the remainder in a conical sieve or strainer. Reserve the court-bouillon.

VEGETABLE ESSENCE

The "essence" of vegetables is the concentration of flavor that can be derived from one vegetable; for example, an essence of celery can be produced. Different vegetables can be used to obtain an essence by cooking the vegetable in water. At the end of the cooking, reduce the liquid.

FISH VELOUTÉ

500 ml (2 cups) fish stock
White roux (see recipe below)
60 g (1/4 cup) butter
160 ml (2/3 cup) 35% cream
Salt and pepper

• In a saucepan, heat the fish stock. Add the cold white roux little by little and cook 10 minutes until the desired consistency is obtained. Add the butter, cream, salt and pepper. Put through a colander or a drum sieve.

WHITE ROUX

480 g (2 cups) butter
480 g (3 1/4 cups) flour

• Melt the butter in the oven or microwave, add the flour, and mix well.

Cook in 20-second sequences and stir well between each sequence. The roux is ready when the mixture begins to bubble.

NOTE: A roux is used by professional chefs and also in home cooking. A roux may also be made in the microwave. It will keep refrigerated for at least a month and may be used when needed. A roux is superior to a beurre manié, as it is cooked.

Using a Thermometer in Modern Cooking

When I first learned my trade, 50 years ago, our chef taught us cooking "by touch." Today it is imperative to use a thermometer to cook food to precise temperatures. It's important to understand that fish never have the same thickness, and the times given are always approximate. All the recipes in this book are based on reaching a temperature of 68°C (155°F) in the center of the fish. However, Dr. Pierre Gélinas in his book ***Répertoire des microorganismes pathogènes***, tells us that we can cook fish to 80°C (180°F) **and reach 52°C (125°F) in the center** of the fish without any problem. It is up to us to decide, based on the quality of the fish and the temperature at which it should be cooked.

	Fresh Fish		Frozen Fish			
	0°C to 4°C 32°F to 40°F	Fresh 4°C to 10°C 40°F to 50°F	Fresh Frozen 0°C to 40°C 32°F to 104°F	Flash Frozen -10°C to -18°C 14°F to -4°F	Flash Frozen -18°C to -25°C -4°F to -13°F	Flash Frozen -30°C -22°F
Storage Time for Fatty Fish	4 to 10 days	none	2 months	4 months	8 months	12 months
Storage Time for lean Fish	4 to 10 days	none	1 ½ months	8 months	18 months	24 months
Storage Time for Flat Fish	4 to 10 days	none	4 months	10 months	24 months	23 months
Development of Pathogenic Bacteria[1]	Slow	Rapid	Stop	Stop	Stop	Stop
Development of Deterioration of Bacteria[2]	Fairly Slow	Very Fast	Very Slow	Stop	Stop	Stop
Chemical Reactions: Tanning and Rancidity[3]	–	–	Fairly Fast	Slow	Very Slow	Very Slow

NOTES: STORAGE TIME FOR FRESH AND FROZEN FISH
1. Pathogenic bacteria: This bacteria produces toxins that may lead to food poisoning.
2. Deterioration bacteria: These produce waste that alters the taste, smell, and appearance of the food and reduces their storage time.
3. Chemical reactions such as brown spots and rancidity can be caused by poor methods of freezing, flash-freezing, or poor packaging. The fish may show a brownish color on its thinner parts.

FISH STOCK

22 ml (1 1/2 tbsp) butter
800 g (1 3/4 lbs) fish bones and trimmings
 (preferably flat fish)
75 g (3/4 cup) onions, finely sliced
125 g (1 1/4 cups) leeks, finely sliced
125 g (1 1/4 cups) celery, finely sliced
90 ml (6 tbsp) shallots, finely sliced
150 g (2 1/2 cups) mushrooms, finely sliced
125 ml (1/2 cup) dry white wine
20 ml (4 tsp) fresh lemon juice
1 litre (4 cups) cold water
1 pinch thyme
1/2 bay leaf
10 peppercorns

• In a saucepan, heat the butter. Sweat (cook on low) the fish bones and trimmings and all the vegetables for 4 to 5 minutes. Add the wine, lemon juice, cold water; add the thyme, bay leaf, and peppercorns. Bring to the boil and then simmer 25 minutes. Pour all ingredients into a conical sieve and reserve the fish stock for future use.

NOTE: The stock may be frozen for 3 to 4 months. Do not use carrots in the preparation of a fish stock as this gives a sweet flavor to the bouillon. Never add salt to a stock as some recipes call for it to be reduced to a concentrated form.

COURT-BOUILLON

A court-bouillon is not often used. However, it is a high quality aromatic base for poaching fish (small or large pieces).

2.5 litres (10 cups) water
125 ml (1/2 cup) white wine
125 ml (1/2 cup) good quality white wine vinegar
30 ml (2 tbsp) coarse salt
300 g (2 cups) onions, finely sliced
300 g (2 2/3 cups) carrots, finely sliced
1 bouquet garni
10 peppercorns

• In a saucepan, place all the ingredients and cook until the carrots and onions are tender. If the court-bouillon is used immediately, reserve the carrots as a garnish for fish or shellfish and strain the remainder in a conical sieve or strainer. Reserve the court-bouillon.

VEGETABLE ESSENCE

The "essence" of vegetables is the concentration of flavor that can be derived from one vegetable; for example, an essence of celery can be produced. Different vegetables can be used to obtain an essence by cooking the vegetable in water. At the end of the cooking, reduce the liquid.

FISH VELOUTÉ

500 ml (2 cups) fish stock
White roux (see recipe below)
60 g (1/4 cup) butter
160 ml (2/3 cup) 35% cream
Salt and pepper

• In a saucepan, heat the fish stock. Add the cold white roux little by little and cook 10 minutes until the desired consistency is obtained. Add the butter, cream, salt and pepper. Put through a colander or a drum sieve.

WHITE ROUX

480 g (2 cups) butter
480 g (3 1/4 cups) flour

• Melt the butter in the oven or microwave, add the flour, and mix well.

Cook in 20-second sequences and stir well between each sequence. The roux is ready when the mixture begins to bubble.

NOTE: A roux is used by professional chefs and also in home cooking. A roux may also be made in the microwave. It will keep refrigerated for at least a month and may be used when needed. A roux is superior to a beurre manié, as it is cooked.

The Basics of Successful Fish Recipes

FISH STOCK

22 ml (1 1/2 tbsp) butter
800 g (1 3/4 lbs) fish bones and trimmings (preferably flat fish)
75 g (3/4 cup) onions, finely sliced
125 g (1 1/4 cups) leeks, finely sliced
125 g (1 1/4 cups) celery, finely sliced
90 ml (6 tbsp) shallots, finely sliced
150 g (2 1/2 cups) mushrooms, finely sliced
125 ml (1/2 cup) dry white wine
20 ml (4 tsp) fresh lemon juice
1 litre (4 cups) cold water
1 pinch thyme
1/2 bay leaf
10 peppercorns

• In a saucepan, heat the butter. Sweat (cook on low) the fish bones and trimmings and all the vegetables for 4 to 5 minutes. Add the wine, lemon juice, cold water; add the thyme, bay leaf, and peppercorns. Bring to the boil and then simmer 25 minutes. Pour all ingredients into a conical sieve and reserve the fish stock for future use.

NOTE: The stock may be frozen for 3 to 4 months. Do not use carrots in the preparation of a fish stock as this gives a sweet flavor to the bouillon. Never add salt to a stock as some recipes call for it to be reduced to a concentrated form.

COURT-BOUILLON

A court-bouillon is not often used. However, it is a high quality aromatic base for poaching fish (small or large pieces).

2.5 litres (10 cups) water
125 ml (1/2 cup) white wine
125 ml (1/2 cup) good quality white wine vinegar
30 ml (2 tbsp) coarse salt
300 g (2 cups) onions, finely sliced
300 g (2 2/3 cups) carrots, finely sliced
1 bouquet garni
10 peppercorns

• In a saucepan, place all the ingredients and cook until the carrots and onions are tender. If the court-bouillon is used immediately, reserve the carrots as a garnish for fish or shellfish and strain the remainder in a conical sieve or strainer. Reserve the court-bouillon.

VEGETABLE ESSENCE

The "essence" of vegetables is the concentration of flavor that can be derived from one vegetable; for example, an essence of celery can be produced. Different vegetables can be used to obtain an essence by cooking the vegetable in water. At the end of the cooking, reduce the liquid.

FISH VELOUTÉ

500 ml (2 cups) fish stock
White roux (see recipe below)
60 g (1/4 cup) butter
160 ml (2/3 cup) 35% cream
Salt and pepper

• In a saucepan, heat the fish stock. Add the cold white roux little by little and cook 10 minutes until the desired consistency is obtained. Add the butter, cream, salt and pepper. Put through a colander or a drum sieve.

WHITE ROUX

480 g (2 cups) butter
480 g (3 1/4 cups) flour

• Melt the butter in the oven or microwave, add the flour, and mix well.

Cook in 20-second sequences and stir well between each sequence. The roux is ready when the mixture begins to bubble.

NOTE: A roux is used by professional chefs and also in home cooking. A roux may also be made in the microwave. It will keep refrigerated for at least a month and may be used when needed. A roux is superior to a beurre manié, as it is cooked.

Using a Thermometer in Modern Cooking

When I first learned my trade, 50 years ago, our chef taught us cooking "by touch." Today it is imperative to use a thermometer to cook food to precise temperatures. It's important to understand that fish never have the same thickness, and the times given are always approximate. All the recipes in this book are based on reaching a temperature of 68°C (155°F) in the center of the fish. However, Dr. Pierre Gélinas in his book *Répertoire des microorganismes pathogènes*, tells us that we can cook fish to 80°C (180°F) **and reach 52°C (125°F) in the center** of the fish without any problem. It is up to us to decide, based on the quality of the fish and the temperature at which it should be cooked.

	Fresh Fish		Frozen Fish			
	0°C to 4°C 32°F to 40°F	Fresh 4°C to 10°C 40°F to 50°F	Fresh Frozen 0°C to 40°C 32°F to 104°F	Flash Frozen -10°C to -18°C 14°F to -4°F	Flash Frozen -18°C to -25°C -4°F to -13°F	Flash Frozen -30°C -22°F
Storage Time for Fatty Fish	4 to 10 days	none	2 months	4 months	8 months	12 months
Storage Time for lean Fish	4 to 10 days	none	1 ½ months	8 months	18 months	24 months
Storage Time for Flat Fish	4 to 10 days	none	4 months	10 months	24 months	23 months
Development of Pathogenic Bacteria[1]	Slow	Rapid	Stop	Stop	Stop	Stop
Development of Deterioration of Bacteria[2]	Fairly Slow	Very Fast	Very Slow	Stop	Stop	Stop
Chemical Reactions: Tanning and Rancidity[3]	–	–	Fairly Fast	Slow	Very Slow	Very Slow

NOTES: STORAGE TIME FOR FRESH AND FROZEN FISH

1. Pathogenic bacteria: This bacteria produces toxins that may lead to food poisoning.
2. Deterioration bacteria: These produce waste that alters the taste, smell, and appearance of the food and reduces their storage time.
3. Chemical reactions such as brown spots and rancidity can be caused by poor methods of freezing, flash-freezing, or poor packaging. The fish may show a brownish color on its thinner parts.

BEURRE BLANC
(WHITE BUTTER)

Juice of 1 lemon
45 ml (3 tbsp) white wine
Salt and white pepper
200 g (3/4 cup) butter, melted

- In a steel bowl, over the bottom of a double boiler, heat lemon juice and white wine, add the salt and pepper, and whisk vigorosly. Incorporate the warm butter.

NOTE: Always add salt and pepper before the butter so the acidity of the wine and lemon juice dissolve the salt and pepper before the butter is added. Beurre blanc is simple to prepare and should be served immediately, unlike beurre nantais, because it has no binding ingredient such as cream.

BEURRE NANTAIS
(NANTAIS BUTTER)

2 shallots, finely chopped
80 ml (1/3 cup) white wine vinegar
Salt and freshly ground pepper
175 ml (3/4 cup) 35% cream
200 g (3/4 cup) cold unsalted butter

- In a saucepan, place shallots, vinegar, white wine vinegar, salt and pepper. Reduce by three-quarters on high heat. Add cream and reduce the mixture by one-half. Gradually add the butter while stirring constantly with a whisk. Remove the saucepan from the heat as soon as the butter is incorporated. Store in refrigerator.

HOLLANDAISE SAUCE
(QUICK METHOD)

There are two methods for making Hollandaise sauce. You can use either the quick or classic method, but the latter produces a superior result.

180 g (3/4 cup) unsalted butter
4 egg yolks
45 ml (3 tbsp) white wine
Salt and pepper
Juice of 1/2 lemon (optional)

- In a saucepan, melt butter.
- In a stainless steel or Pyrex bowl, using a whisk, beat egg yolks, white wine, salt and pepper.
- Set in the bottom half of a double boiler containing warm water, and whisk the mixture until it forms a ribbon (thick, like whipped cream). This step is very important because it is the emulsion of the egg yolks with the acids that makes for the success of this sauce.
- Once the desired consistency is obtained, incorporate the melted butter a bit at a time. The mixture should be creamy. If necessary, add more lemon juice.

NOTE: Always use unsalted butter as it is a denser fat.

HOLLANDAISE SAUCE
(CLASSIC METHOD)

80 ml (1/3 cup) white wine
75 ml (5 tbsp) shallots, chopped
10 ml (2 tsp) white wine vinegar
4 egg yolks
Salt and pepper
180 g (3/4 cup) unsalted butter
Juice of 1/2 lemon (optional)

- In a saucepan, place the wine, shallots, and vinegar and reduce by nine-tenths. Let cool and add egg yolks. Put through a very fine sieve.
- In a small pan, melt butter.
- In a stainless steel or Pyrex bowl, whisk the egg mixture and white wine. Add salt and pepper.
- Over the bottom half of a double boiler containing warm water, whisk the mixture until it forms a ribbon (thick, like whipped cream). This step is very important because it is the emulsion of the egg yolks with the acidity of the white wine that makes for the success of this sauce. When the desired consistency is obtained, gradually beat in the butter. The mixture should be creamy. If necessary, add the lemon juice.

NOTE: Always use unsalted butter as it is a denser fat.

BÉARNAISE SAUCE

45 ml (3 tbsp) white wine vinegar
80 ml (1/3 cup) white wine
10 ml (2 tsp) peppercorns
15 ml (1 tbsp) fresh tarragon, chopped
60 ml (4 tbsp) shallots, chopped
300 g (1 1/4 cups) melted butter
3 egg yolks
Salt and pepper
15 ml (1 tbsp) tarragon, chopped for garnish
15 ml (1 tbsp) parsley, chopped for garnish
15 ml (1 tbsp) chives, chopped for garnish

• Pour the vinegar and wine into a saucepan, add pepper, tarragon, and shallots. Reduce by half and let cool.
• Melt butter in a heavy pan over low heat. Pour the warm clarified butter into a second pan, leaving behind the milky residue, and keep warm.
• Put the vinegar and wine reduction and the egg yolks in a stainless steel or Pyrex bowl over the bottom of a double boiler and whisk until thick and creamy. Gently incorporate the clarified butter, making sure that the butter is not too hot.
• Rub the reduced sauce through a drum sieve and season to taste. If the sauce is too thick, add a little warm water to thin slightly. Garnish with chopped tarragon, parsley, and chives and serve.

NOTE : Béarnaise sauce is a hollandaise sauce using the classic method of preparation to which chopped tarragon and chives are added. The finished sauce is not sieved again.

FINE HERBES SAUCE WITH CRAYFISH

16 raw crayfish, shell on
45 ml (3 tbsp) oil
325 g (3 1/2 cups) onions, chopped
30 ml (2 tbsp) shallots, finely chopped
45 ml (3 tbsp) carrots, chopped
1 pinch thyme
1 bay leaf
80 ml (1/3 cup) cognac
375 ml (1 1/2 cups) fish stock, heated
 (see recipe pg. 12)
175 ml (3/4 cup) white wine
Salt and pepper
1 pinch cayenne
60 g (1/4 cup) butter
100 g (2/3 cup) flour
125 ml (1/2 cup) 35% cream

FINES HERBES

5 ml (1 tsp) chives, chopped
5 ml (1 tsp) parsley, chopped
2 1/2 ml (1/2 tsp) tarragon, chopped

• Clean the crayfish. (Keep the shell on, but remove the digestive tract. The tail of the crayfish is composed of three sections. Hold the middle section between two fingers and gently give a quarter turn. The long black filament should come out in one piece.)
• In a skillet, heat the oil on high heat, brown the vegetables and crayfish with the thyme and bay leaf.
• When the crayfish turn red, flambé with cognac, and pour in the hot fish stock and white wine. Season and cook for 12 minutes.
• Remove the crayfish from the skillet. Remove the shells, but do not discard, and keep crayfish tails to decorate the platter.
• Return the carcass and shells to the skillet and rub the hot mixture through a conical sieve or strainer. Keep the liquid hot.
• Prepare a roux with butter and flour (see recipe pg. 12). Add the hot liquid and thicken while stirring with a wooden spoon. Let simmer, stirring constantly, for 8 minutes. Add the cream to liquid. Cook until the sauce is very creamy. Add fines herbes and correct seasonings.

LOBSTER OR CRAB STOCK

500 g (approx 1 lb) lobster or crab
60 ml (1/4 cup) oil
60 g (1/2 cup) carrots, cubed
45 ml (3 tbsp) onions, cubed
45 ml (3 tbsp) celery, cubed
25 g (1/4 cup) white part of leeks, cubed
100 g (1/2 cup) fresh tomatoes, cubed
20 ml (4 tsp) cognac
1 litre (4 cups) fish stock (see recipe pg. 12)
20 ml (4 tsp) tomato paste
2 cloves garlic
1 pinch thyme, chopped
1 bay leaf
Salt and pepper

• Chop the lobster very coarsely in its shell, removing the stomach and intestines.
• Sear the lobster chunks in the oil. Add vegetables and cook 4 to 5 minutes.
• Pour off oil and flambé with cognac. Moisten with fish stock. Add the tomato paste, garlic, thyme, bay leaf, salt and pepper. Simmer for 30 minutes.
• Crush or finely chop the lobster and vegetables, and rub through a conical sieve or strainer. Simmer 1 to 2 minutes and adjust seasonings to taste.

NOTE: This stock can be frozen; it can also be prepared with crab carcasses.

LOBSTER COULIS

900 g (2 lbs) lobster
60 ml (1/4 cup) olive oil
60 ml (4 tbsp) unsalted butter
30 ml (2 tbsp) shallots, chopped
1/2 garlic clove, green center removed, chopped
125 ml (1/2 cup) cognac
175 ml (3/4 cup) white wine
160 ml (2/3 cup) fish stock (see recipe pg. 12)
30 ml (2 tbsp) tomato paste
15 ml (1 tbsp) fresh parsley, coarsely chopped
80 ml (1/3 cup) demi-glace
Cayenne and salt

• Cut the lobster tail into 3 or 4 slices and break off or cut off the large claws. Crack the claws in two, lengthwise. Remove the pouch of gravel (stomach) located between the eyes and discard. Reserve the creamy part (roe), if any, and the flesh.
• In a heavy lidded, heat-proof casserole dish, heat the oil and butter on medium heat, add the lobster parts, and sear until the lobster shells are bright red. Drain off the fat and add all remaining ingredients.
• Place lid on casserole and continue cooking in the oven.
• Remove lobster pieces, extract lobster meat, and set aside for another use.
• Crush the shells and return them to the sauce with the creamy parts of the lobster. Cook on medium to high heat until reduced, stirring constantly. Rub through a conical sieve or strainer, reserving the liquid.

NOTE: This recipe can be made by replacing the lobster with crab, large shrimp, or crayfish.

LOBSTER BISQUE

80 g (1/3 cup) butter
30 g (1/4 cup) carrots, cubed
30 g (1/4 cup) onions, cubed
30 g (1/4 cup) celery, cubed
45 g (1/2 cup) white part of leek, cubed
20 ml (4 tsp) cognac
60 ml (1/4 cup) white wine
30 ml (2 tbsp) tomato paste
200 g (1/3 cup) fresh tomatoes, cubed
800 g (1 3/4 lbs) lobster shells
750 ml (3 cups) fish stock (see recipe pg. 12)
750 ml (3 cups) white chicken stock (see recipe pg. 17)
Salt and pepper
Cayenne
90 g (3 oz) lobster meat
Rice flour
80 ml (1/3 cup) 35% cream

• In a saucepan, heat butter and cook the carrots, onions, celery, and leeks until soft. Deglaze the pan with the cognac and white wine. Add tomato paste and fresh tomatoes. Add lobster shells. Add the fish stock and white chicken stock. Season and simmer for 1 hour.

• Pour all ingredients into a colander or strainer, reserving the liquid. Gently cook the lobster meat in the strained liquid. Mix rice flour with cream and stir into the hot liquid. Stir until desired thickness. Again, rub mixture through a conical sieve or strainer, reserving the bisque. Remove the cooked lobster, dice, and add to strained bisque.

NOTES: When is the word bisque used? It is used when the base of the sauce is shellfish (crayfish, crab, shrimp, lobster, etc.). To thicken a bisque, always use rice flour, as it is tasteless and doesn't alter the delicate shellfish flavour.
It is possible to find commercially prepared lobster bisques of good quality. You can also buy crab, shrimp, and crayfish bisques. Also available are demi-glace, hollandaise, and béarnaise sauces, and veal stock. However, these commercially prepared products do not compare with the quality of a fresh, homemade sauce.

LOBSTER SAUCE

900 g (2 lbs) lobster or lobster shells
45 ml (3 tbsp) olive oil
30 ml (2 tbsp) shallots, chopped
1 ml (1/4 tsp) garlic, chopped
125 ml (1/2 cup) cognac
80 ml (1/3 cup) white wine
830 ml (3 1/3 cups) fish stock (see recipe pg. 12)
30 ml (2 tbsp) tomato paste
15 ml (1 tbsp) parsley, coarsely chopped
2 ml (1/2 tsp) cayenne
2 ml (1/2 tsp) salt

• Cut the lobster tail into slices, break off the claws and crack in two, lengthwise. Remove the pouch of gravel (stomach) located between the eyes and discard. Reserve the creamy parts (roe) and the flesh.
• In a large skillet, heat oil and sear the lobster pieces on medium high until the shells turn red. Pour off any fat and add remaining ingredients.
• Cover and cook at 200–230°C (400–450°F) for approximately 30 minutes. Remove the lobster shell chunks, pound them, and return to the sauce with creamy parts and lobster flesh. Cook on medium high heat and reduce while stirring. Rub through a conical sieve or strainer and reserve the sauce, refrigerated, until needed.

LOBSTER BUTTER

480 g (1 lb) soft lobster shells (head, body, little claws, coral, but not the large claws)
480 g (2 cups) soft unsalted butter
Ice water

• Crush the soft shell parts with a pestle or in a food processor, add the butter and blend until smooth. Put the butter mixture in the top of a double boiler and heat on low for 30 minutes.
• Pour approximately 2.5 cm (1") ice water in the bottom of a tall, narrow container.
• Pour the melted butter mixture through a cheese-cloth-lined strainer or a conical sieve placed over the ice water. Press the butter mixture well to extract the maximum amount of melted butter. Leave butter in ice water until all the butter has risen to the surface. Place the whole container in the refrigerator until the butter has congealed.
• Separate the hardened butter from the water. Set on some paper towels to absorb any clinging water, and then melt once again. Transfer the butter to an airtight jar and store in the refrigerator until needed.

NOTE: Store the butter in the refrigerator where it will keep for several weeks. Use for canapés, to decorate cold dishes, and to enrich fish or shellfish sauces. If desired, replace the lobster with other shellfish (crab, crayfish, shrimp). This butter may be frozen.

WHITE CHICKEN STOCK

2 kg (4 1/2 lbs) chicken bones
300 g (3 cups) carrots, small dice
200 g (2 cups) onions, small dice
100 g (1 cup) white part of leeks, small dice
110 g (1 cup) celery, medium dice
3 cloves garlic, chopped
1 clove
Black pepper
1 bouquet garni of 20 parsley sprigs, 1 sprig thyme, and 1/2 bay leaf

• Degorge (sprinkle with salt and leave for 1/2 to 1 hour) and rinse the chicken bones.
• In a large stock pot, place the degorged bones and remaining ingredients.
• Cover with water and bring to the boil. Skim off scum if necessary. Simmer the chicken bones for 45 minutes. Rub through a conical sieve or a fine strainer into a large pot, reserving the stock. Reduce stock until desired flavour is obtained.

NOTE: This recipe can be made using any poultry bones. The base ingredients remain the same. If using a whole chicken, simmer the bird whole; as the cooking is longer, the result is a richer flavour. If chicken bones are used, degorge them to remove any impurities (blood).

BROWN CHICKEN STOCK

In certain recipes, a brown chicken stock is called for. To make it, the ingredients are the same as for the white chicken stock, but the method is slightly different.

With a cleaver, chop the chicken bones into several pieces. Braise in the oven at 200°C (400°F) on a baking sheet with a little oil, until the bones become golden brown. Meanwhile, sweat the vegetables in oil. Next, put the bones and vegetables together in the stock pot with the seasonings. Cover with water and simmer 45 to 60 minutes. If the stock is not sufficiently colored, add a little tomato paste. Rub mixture through a conical sieve or large strainer.

BROWN VEAL STOCK

Brown veal stock was very popular with fish and shellfish in the sixteenth, seventeenth, and eighteenth centuries. Fortunately, stocks can be made any time, i.e., in the winter, frozen, and used later. As they cook, they send a wonderful aroma throughout the house and add humidity to a dry winter home.

Vegetable oil
10 kg (22 lbs) veal bones, preferably veal knuckle, diced by the butcher
Vegetable oil
1 kg (2 1/4 lbs) onions, coarsely chopped
1 kg (2 1/4 lbs) carrots, coarsely chopped
480 g (1 lb) celery stalk, cut into 5 cm (2") pieces
2 whole garlic bulbs in skin
1 bay leaf
2 pinches thyme
200 g (6 1/2 cups) parsley
25 black peppercorns
200 g (7 oz) tomato paste

• Heat vegetable oil in a roasting pan in a 200°C (400°F) oven. When well heated, add veal bones and oven roast until they are browned on all sides. This is an important step since it is the browned pan juices that give the lovely brown color to the stock.
• Meanwhile, in a large saucepan, sweat the vegetables in hot vegetable oil, add garlic, seasonings, and tomato paste, and cook until tender.
• When the bones and vegetables are cooked, combine both in a stock pot, cover with water, bring to the boil, and then simmer for at least 6 hours.
• By reducing the stock, there is a concentration of flavor, and a demi-glace sauce is obtained. A veal glaze is obtained with further intensive reduction.
• This veal stock is not thick. To obtain a thickened brown sauce, use a white roux (see recipe pg. 12).

GLAZES

Meat glazes contain concentrated flavor and are used to lend body to sauces. To obtain a glaze, reduce a poultry, veal or fish stock by 95%. For example, 5 litres (20 cups) of chicken stock must be cooked 40 to 60 minutes, rubbed through a conical sieve or fine strainer, then reduced by 90–95%. This leaves 250–500 ml (1–2 cups) of liquid, producing a very concentrated glaze. If you stop the reduction at 1 litre (4 cups) of liquid, the glaze will have less flavor. Once you have made the glaze, pour it into ice cube trays and freeze. When frozen, remove from trays and store in small bags. When a sauce lacks flavor, add a cube of glaze.

GARLIC CREAM

Generally, garlic is not used in the preparation of most fish dishes; however, certain dishes, such as shellfish, are complemented by its addition. Garlic cream is simply 35% cream whipped into garlic butter.

GARLIC BUTTER

480 g (1 lb) unsalted butter
30 g (1/3 cup) fresh garlic
30 g (1/3 cup) shallots or onions
60 g (2 cups) parsley
15 ml (1 tbsp) Dijon mustard
30 ml (2 tbsp) toasted almonds
30 ml (2 tbsp) Pernod or Ricard liqueur
Salt and pepper

• Blend all ingredients in a food processor. Salt and pepper to taste.

FISH BASED MOUSSE

1 kg (2 1/4 lbs) pike, flounder, or bluefish
4–5 egg whites
Salt and fresh ground pepper
Nutmeg
1 litre (4 cups) 35% cream
375 g (2 1/2 cups) unsalted butter

• Mash fish flesh by pulsing in a food processor.
• Add egg whites and seasoning while machine is running. Rub through a conical sieve or fine strainer and proceed with method for conserving (storing) fresh fish, (pg. 8). Leave on ice for approximately 2 hours.
• Using a wooden spoon, gently stir butter and cream into the ground fish mixture while on ice. Let chill overnight before using.

PANADE FOR FISH

115 g (3/4 cup) flour
4 egg yolks
80 g (1/3 cup) melted butter
Salt, pepper, nutmeg
250 ml (1 cup) milk

• In a saucepan, mix flour and egg yolks. Add melted butter, salt, pepper, and nutmeg to taste.
• In a separate saucepan, bring the milk to a boil and slowly stir it into the mixture, mixing vigorously. Simmer for 6 to 8 minutes, stirring with a whisk. As soon as the mixture thickens, remove from heat and refrigerate.

STUFFING FOR QUENELLES

1 kg (2 1/4 lbs) pike
5 egg whites
Salt, fresh ground pepper
2 1/2 ml (1/2 tsp) nutmeg, freshly grated
400 g (14 oz) puff pastry dough
1 litre (4 cups) 35% cream
225 g (3/4–1 cup) soft unsalted butter
2 litres (8 cups) fish stock (see recipe pg. 12)

• Ask your fishmonger to prepare pike fillets. Cut them into small pieces and reduce to a purée in a food processor along with the egg whites and seasonings.
• Transfer mixture to a large bowl and add puff pastry dough. Mix well.

Press through a fine sieve in the large bowl of a standing electric mixer, and blend with the dough hook on low speed.

• Gradually incorporate the cream and soft butter. Increase the speed and whip approximately 1 minute until a creamy smooth stuffing is obtained. Refrigerate overnight.

• Form the quenelles in the shape of a large egg, using 2 dampened spoons and approximately 90 g (3 oz) of stuffing. Place in a large, shallow buttered cake or baking dish.

• Cover carefully with fish stock and bake approximately 10 minutes at 150°C (300°F), basting from time to time.

• Drain the quenelles, set liquid aside, and return to oven until stuffing has thickened.

MAYONNAISE

4 egg yolks
15 ml (1 tbsp) Dijon mustard
Salt and white pepper
White wine vinegar (good quality)
1 litre (4 cups) oil of choice (olive, peanut, canola, corn, sunflower, walnut, etc.)

• In a food processor, blender, or with a whisk, mix egg yolks well with mustard, salt, pepper, and a few drops of vinegar. It is important to add the salt at this point so that it dissolves. Then add the oil, a few drops at a time to begin with, and build to a fine stream. If the mayonnaise becomes too thick, add a few drops of vinegar or water to thin out mixture before adding more oil.

LEMON HERB BUTTER

160 g (2/3 cup) unsalted butter
30 ml (2 tbsp) fresh lemon juice
20 g (2/3 cup) parsley, chopped
20 g (1/2 cup) chives, chopped
10 g (1/3 cup) tarragon, chopped
Salt and pepper

• Soften butter and mix with remaining ingredients.

• Store butter at room temperature until used. Freeze any leftovers.

NOTE: You can substitute orange or grapefruit juice to achieve a different flavor.

At birth, these fish swim in a normal, upright position but this changes, and they switch to swimming on one side. As a result, the eye that is on the bottom side "migrates" to the same side of the head as the other eye. This change brings about a transformation in the structure of the head, muscle tissues, and nervous system of the flat fish.

Flat fish are carnivorous. They are ocean-floor feeders in continental coastal waters, and are found in abundance in temperate and tropical seas. Some species can be found in arctic waters.

This group has approximately 500 species categorized in six families. Those that we find on the Atlantic coast vary widely in taste; suffice it to say that when you buy sole, you are actually eating flounder; and in this family, the quality of the fish varies according to the name. Unfortunately, all flounder are often grouped together, and when cooked, some filets are nice and firm and others are softer. It is therefore important that you select flounder in the following order: witch flounder, Canadian plaice, yellowtail flounder, red flounder, summer flounder.

Flat Fish

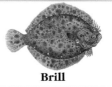 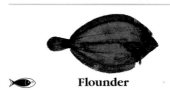
Maximum ★★★★; $$$$$
"Commonly Called" includes nicknames and misnomers

Windowpane

Scientific name: *Scophthalmus aquosus* (Mitchill, 1815). **Commonly called:** plaice, sole. **Characteristics:** Color varying from reddish to brownish grey on one side and plain white on the other side. Average size about 56 cm (22"), and weight from 600 g to 1 kg (1¼ lbs to 2¼ lbs) for a baby, up to 10 kg (22 lbs) for a full-grown windowpane. **Rating:** One of the best fish from the sea, but 60% cannot be used for food. **Quality:** ★★★★★. **Cost:** $$$$$.

Brill

Scientific name: *Scophthalmus rombus* (Linné, 1758). **Commonly called:** sole, turbot. **Characteristics:** Flat fish of oval shape, 50 cm (20"); habitat on sand or gravel. Colored side is greyish, yellowish, or brownish. **Rating:** The quality of brill is one level below that of the windowpane. It can be served whole, in filets or in chunks. Like the Windowpane, 60% is inedible. **Quality:** ★★★★. **Cost:** $$$$.

Common Sole

Scientific name: *Solea solea* and *Solea lascaris* (Risso, 1810). **Commonly called:** flounder, sole, Dover sole. **Characteristics:** There are no common sole on the Canadian East coast. They are found mostly in the North Sea and the English Channel. A very fine fish with a waste of 30%, can be prepared as meunière, poached, or grilled. **Quality:** ★★★★★. **Cost:** $$$$. **Other sole:** Senegal sole (*Solea senegalensis*); Partridge Sole (*Microchirus variegatus*); Céteau sole (*Sicologoglossa*); Tongue Sole (*Cynoglossidae*).

Halibut

Scientific name: *Hippoglossus hippoglossus* (Linné, 1758). **Commonly called:** turbot, windowpane, flounder. **Characteristics:** Halibut is often found with cod in the cold Atlantic waters almost to Antarctica. Its color is brown on one side and white on the other. This fish can reach up to 240 cm (8') long, and could weigh up to 181.5 kg (400 lbs). However, its average weight varies from 2.3 kg to 20 kg (5 lbs to 44 lbs). **Rating:** Unknown or little consumed in Europe, it is a fish of high quality when fresh. It can be served in small or large pieces. **Quality:** ★★★★. **Cost:** $$ to $$$.

Flounder

Scientific name: *Microstomus kitt* (Walbaum, 1792). Commonly called: small mouth sole, flounder, sole. **Characteristics:** Flounder looks very much like the red flounder of the Canadian Atlantic coast (*Pseudopleuronectes americanus* (Walbaum, 1792). Its size varies from 25 cm to 35 cm (10" to 14"). It has an orange marking along the operculum edge. **Rating:** In decreasing order, its culinary value is equal to that of the yellowtail flounder. **Quality:** ★★★. **Cost:** $$$.

Slippery Flounder

Scientific name: *Limanda limanda* (Linné, 1758). **Commonly called:** flounder, sole, Pacific sole. **Characteristics:** Fished in the North Sea and the English Channel, it is found in North America under the name Greenland Flounder (*Reinhardtius hippoglossoides* (Walbaum, 1792). Its weight varies from 450 g to 2 kg (1 lb to 4½ lbs), and its size from 20 cm to 35 cm (8" to15"). **Rating:** Quality is inferior to the witch flounder or flounder. It is, nevertheless, a much appreciated fish. **Quality:** ★★★. **Cost:** $$$.

Witch Flounder

Scientific name: *Glyptocephalus cynoglossus* (Linné, 1758). **Commonly called:** sole, grey sole. **Characteristics:** Fish with lean and firm flesh, brown, greyish body on one side and white-grey with dark spots on the other. Maximum size of 64 cm (25"), and weight approximately 700 g (1½ lbs). **Rating:** Among the small flat fish category it is the best after the common sole. **Quality:** ★★★. **Cost:** $$$.

American Plaice

Scientific name: *Hyppoglossoides platessoides* (Fabricius, 1780). **Commonly called:** sole, flounder, summer flounder. **Characteristics:** This fish of 70 cm (27") can weigh from 900 g to 1.4 kg (2 lbs to 3 lbs). It is the only fish on the Canadian East coast which has a right lateral line, a rounded tail, a large mouth, and eyes on the right side. **Rating:** Of equal quality to the European flounder, it is better than the yellowtail flounder, but not as good as the witch flounder. **Quality:** ★★★. **Cost:** $$$.

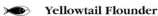

Yellowtail Flounder

Scientific name: *Limanda ferruginea* (Storer, 1839). **Commonly called:** sole. **Characteristics:** Of brownish olive color with orange spots on one side and white on the other, its flesh is lean and soft. The yellowtail flounder can reach 72 cm (28") in length and weigh 600 g (1¼ lbs) for every 40 cm (16") in length. **Rating:** The texture of its flesh makes it more desirable for an informal meal. **Quality:** ★★. **Cost:** $$.

Flounder

Scientific name: *Platichthys flesus* (Linné, 1758). **Commonly called:** sole, flounder, carrelet. **Characteristics:** This fish is 20 cm to 40 cm (8" to 16") on average, and can weigh 500 g to 2 kg (1 lb to 4½ lbs). Its taste is similar to that of the American plaice. **Rating:** As filets, whole, poached, or grilled, it rates somewhat behind the common sole. **Quality:** ★★★. **Cost:** $$$.

Summer Flounder

Scientific name: *Paralichthys oblongus* (Mitchill, 1815). **Commonly called:** flounder, windowpane, turbot, sole. **Characteristics:** Summer flounder can be recognized by its 4 markings. Its length can reach 110 cm (43") and can weigh 115 kg (25 lbs), but its average weight is from 600 g to 1.2 kg (1½ lbs to 2½ lbs). Its average length is between 25 cm and 35 cm (10" to 14"). **Rating:** Everyday fish, its flesh is not firm. **Quality:** ★★. **Cost:** $$.

Plaice

Scientific name: *Pleuronectes platessa* (Linné, 1758). **Commonly called:** common flounder, summer flounder. **Characteristics:** Close cousin to the summer flounder, it measures from 25 cm to 65 cm (10" to 26"), and its flesh is rather soft, making it a fish of lesser quality. **Quality:** ★★. **Cost:** $$.

Champagne Filets of Windowpane, Lobster Medallions, and Truffles

4 servings · Difficulty: 2 · Preparation: 30 min · Cooking time: 20 min

Windowpane is considered one of the best salt water fish for eating. For an aristocratic fish, what better to accompany it with than champagne? We do not have this fish in our Canadian Atlantic waters, so substitute with a very fresh halibut.

Don't be confused: *the fish called turbot is the Greenland halibut and doesn't compare to the Atlantic Boreal halibut.*

• Choose an oven-proof baking dish large enough to accommodate the halibut when placed side by side. Using a pastry brush, coat the bottom of the dish with 60 g (¼ cup) butter and sprinkle with shallots.

• Salt and pepper the halibut filets and place one beside the other in the dish.

• Preheat oven to 180°C (350°F).

• Pour champagne and fish stock over fish, cover with parchment paper, and bake in oven until it reaches 68°C (155°F) at its thickest part.

• Remove filets, place on absorbent paper, and keep hot.

• Reduce the resulting liquid by 90% and stir in the cream. Adjust seasonings and pour through a strainer.

VEGETABLE ACCOMPANIMENTS

Potatoes cooked in water.

INGREDIENTS

- 60 g (¼ cup) unsalted butter
- 2 shallots, chopped finely
- Salt and fresh ground white pepper
- 4 halibut filets 150 g (5 oz) each
- 375 ml (1 ½ cups) champagne brut
- 175 ml (¾ cup) fish stock (see recipe pg. 12)
- 250 ml (1 cup) 35% cream
- 80 g (⅓ cup) unsalted butter
- 4 truffle slices
- 4 lobster medallions

INFORMATION

"White" is the modern nomenclature for a thick halibut filet.

ALTERNATIVE FISH CHOICES

Fresh halibut, brill, sole, and John Dory filet.

TIPS

The best fish stock is made with the fish heads and bones of flat fish.

SERVING SUGGESTIONS

Place the filets on heated plates and nappe (cover) with the champagne sauce. Garnish with truffle slices and lobster medallions.

Grilled Halibut
with Hollandaise Sauce

4 servings • Difficulty: 3 • Preparation: 10 min • Cooking time: 12 to 15 min

- 4 slices of halibut 150 g to 180 g (5 oz to 6 oz) each
- Salt and fresh ground pepper
- 80 ml (⅓ cup) sunflower oil
- 250 ml (1 cup) hollandaise sauce (see basic recipe pg. 13), or olive oil and lemon emulsion

SERVING SUGGESTIONS

Place halibut steaks on very hot dinner plates, garnish with vegetables, and serve the sauce separately.

Fish or meat should be grilled, not burnt. Blackened grilled food gives a bitter flavor to the finished product.

- In order to have a successfully grilled fish, it must be well dried, so dry each slice well with a clean tea towel or paper towel. Salt and pepper.
- Using a pastry brush, coat each slice with oil. Sear each side on high heat, turning to form squares on the flesh, then reduce heat to medium for a few minutes and finish grilling on low. When the temperature of each slice reaches 68°C (155°F), the fish will be cooked to perfection. It should have a short resting time before serving.

OLIVE OIL AND LEMON EMULSION

Pour lemon juice into blender, or food processor, add salt, fresh ground white pepper, and incorporate 250 ml (1 cup) olive oil in a fine stream.

VEGETABLE ACCOMPANIMENTS

Sliced sweet potatoes, blanched and grilled, and grilled yellow peppers.

TECHNIQUE

Whether a stove-top grill or a barbecue is used, it is important to follow these three steps:

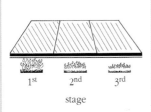

1st   2nd   3rd

stage

TERMINOLOGY

Why a "slice" and not a "steak"? The word steak is associated with beef, so in culinary terms, the word slice is used for flat fish, but steak is used for a crescent shape (eg., salmon steak).

Cutting a slice.   A slice of flat fish.   Cutting a steak.   A salmon steak.

Plaice Asparagus Rolls

4 servings · Difficulty: 4 · Preparation: 20 min · Cooking time: 8 to 10 min

PREPARATION

INGREDIENTS

- Preheat oven to 150°C (300°F).

- Salt and pepper the plaice filets.

- Cut asparagus so that the stems are the length of the filets with asparagus tips protruding, and roll in the filet.

- Coat the bottom of an oven-proof pan with 60 g (¼ cup) butter and sprinkle with chopped shallots and dried seaweed.

- Place rolled filets in the pan and pour white wine and fish stock over all. Cover with buttered parchment paper and a lid.

- Bake just until the filets begin to flake.

- Remove filets, place on absorbent paper, and keep hot. Pour the cooking juices into the bowl of a standing electric mixer and incorporate the veal pan juices, or veal stock, and sunflower oil or soft butter. Adjust seasonings.

VEGETABLE ACCOMPANIMENTS

Creole rice or pilaf mixed with asparagus tips, or couscous.

- 12 plaice filets 60 g (2 oz) each
- Salt and fresh ground white pepper
- 36 green asparagus stalks, cooked or canned
- 60 g (¼ cup) soft unsalted butter
- 3 shallots, finely chopped
- 30 g (1 oz) dehydrated seaweed
- 175 ml (¾ cup) dry white wine
- 175 ml (¾ cup) fish stock (see recipe pg. 12)
- 160 ml (⅔ cup) veal pan juices or veal stock
- 60 ml (¼ cup) sunflower oil or 60 g (¼ cup) softened unsalted butter (room temperature)

ALTERNATIVE FISH CHOICES

Any flat fish except halibut, turbot, or brill.

SERVING SUGGESTIONS

Place the fish rolls on heated dinner plates and nappe (cover) with the sauce.

TECHNIQUE

Prepare the filets the following way:

Place the filets between two sheets of foil.	Tap gently to extend the filet.	Large filet.
Place asparagus tip on extended filet.	Roll carefully.	Roll is ready to cook.

INGREDIENTS

- 210 g (7 oz) raw shrimp
- Salt and fresh ground pepper
- ½ egg white
- 125 ml (½ cup) 35% cream
- 4 sole 180 g to 210 g (6 oz to 7 oz) each
- Salt and fresh ground pepper
- 60 g (¼ cup) unsalted butter, softened to room temperature
- 3 shallots, finely chopped
- 30 g (¼ cup) carrots, finely diced
- 1 celery stalk, finely diced
- 250 ml (1 cup) dry white wine
- 175 ml (¾ cup) fish stock
- 125 ml (½ cup) 35% cream
- 60 g (¼ cup) unsalted butter
- Salt and fresh ground white pepper

ALTERNATIVE FISH CHOICES
Flounder, yellowtail flounder, summer flounder, plaice.

SERVING SUGGESTIONS
Place sole on heated dinner plates and nappe (cover) with the cream sauce.

VEGETABLE ACCOMPANIMENTS
Jerusalem artichoke, bite-sized potatoes boiled in salted butter.

Shrimp Mousseline Stuffed Sole

4 servings · Difficulty: 2 · Preparation: 60 min · Cooking time: by thermometer

- Shell and devein raw shrimp, and set shells aside. Wash and dry shrimp and place in bowl of food processor with salt and pepper. Incorporate the egg white and cream, pulsing just until mixture is combined. Adjust seasonings.

- Spread open the sole and salt and pepper. Using a pastry bag, squeeze shrimp mousseline down one side of filet and gently fold other side over filling.

- Butter broiling pan with 60 g (¼ cup) butter. Place sole, alternating head and tail, in pan, and sprinkle fish with shallots, carrots, celery, shrimp shells, and chopped fish bones (See "Technique" below).

- Pour white wine and fish stock over all. Cover with buttered parchment paper and bake until inserted meat thermometer reaches 68°C (155°F) at thickest part.

- Remove the sole, place on a platter and, while hot, remove the small bones from each side of the filets, using a steel spatula. Reform each fish shape and keep hot, covering with a damp tea towel to avoid drying. Pour cooking juices through a strainer into a saucepan. Set aside the finely chopped cooked vegetables. Add 35% cream to strained fish juices and reduce to desired consistency. Using a whisk, beat in the soft butter. Incorporate the finely chopped cooked vegetables. Adjust seasonings and press through a strainer. Adjust seasonings again if necessary and set sauce aside.

TECHNIQUE

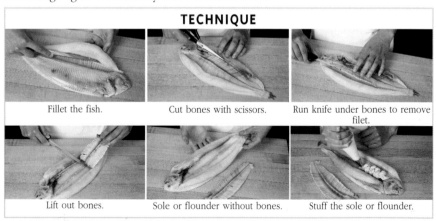

| Fillet the fish. | Cut bones with scissors. | Run knife under bones to remove filet. |
| Lift out bones. | Sole or flounder without bones. | Stuff the sole or flounder. |

Omelette with Plaice Stew
and Sea String Beans

4 servings · Difficulty: 2 · Preparation: 20 min · Cooking time: 20 min

- 210 g (7 oz) plaice (tail end of filets)
- 60 ml (¼ cup) olive oil
- 150 g (5 oz) sea string beans
- 160 ml (⅔ cup) lobster bisque (see recipe pg. 15) or commercial equivalent
- Salt and fresh ground pepper
- 12 eggs, beaten

RAGOÛT DE PLIE

- Ask your fishmonger for the plaice tails as they are less expensive.

- Wipe flesh well and cut into small slices 2 cm x 0.5 cm (¾" x ¼"); salt and pepper.

- Heat oil in an iron pan and sear the fish slices approximately 20 seconds. Drain on paper towelling and keep hot.

- Rinse sea string beans and, if they are too salty, blanch them, drain, and sauté in the same oil as the fish. Drain off cooking oil.

- Mix the sea string beans and plaice, add the lobster bisque. Blend gently, adjust seasonings, and keep hot.

- Salt and pepper the eggs. Cook an omelette, being careful to incorporate the stew in the center. Roll out onto a dish and serve immediately.

VEGETABLE ACCOMPANIMENT

Small potatoes, boiled in salted water, and small carrots with about an inch of the green stem left on.

> **ALTERNATIVE FISH CHOICES**
> Any fish bits from the fishmonger.

> **INFORMATION**
> **Salicornia:** Sea string beans are also known as sea beans. This small tender edible seaweed 16 cm to 23 cm (8" to 10") turns red at the end of the growing season. It grows in very salty areas, and its flavor is reminiscent of the ocean. It is often pickled.

Flat Fish Soup Garnished with Lobster Mousse or Coral Butter Croutons

4 servings · Difficulty: 3 · Preparation: 40 min · Cooking time: 60 min

- 210 g (7 oz) cooked lobster meat (fresh or canned), drained and dried, or lobster coral
- 120 g (½ cup) soft unsalted butter (room temperature)
- 1 baguette sliced lengthwise 0.5 cm (¼") thick
- 80 ml (⅓ cup) olive oil
- 180 g (2 cups) carrots, onions, and celery, diced finely (mirepoix)
- 6 cloves garlic, finely chopped
- 800 g (1¾ lbs) pieces of flat fish (ask your fishmonger for bones and tails)
- 310 ml ((1¼ cups) white wine
- 150 g (5 oz) tomato paste
- 625 ml (2½ cups) fish stock, homemade (see recipe pg. 12) or store bought
- 1 bouquet garni
- 30 g (1 cup) parsley, finely chopped

ALTERNATIVE FISH CHOICES

Fish soup can be made using rock fish, goat fish, red fish, weever, etc., but the following should be avoided: pickerel, pike, barbot, carp, and silure.

SERVING SUGGESTIONS

Pour soup into soup bowls. Garnish with croutons and parsley.

LOBSTER MOUSSE OR CORAL BUTTER[1]

- While chopping the cooked lobster in a food processor, incorporate the butter little by little. Season to taste and leave at room temperature.
- Grill each side of the bread slices at 155°C (310°F). Set aside.

FLAT FISH SOUP

- In a large saucepan, heat the oil, add mirepoix (finely diced vegetables), garlic, and pieces of flat fish. Sweat (heat gently) until fish bits begin to turn white around the bones. Add white wine and tomato paste, and cook 10 minutes.
- Add the fish stock, bouquet garni, and cook a further 15 minutes.
- Using a slotted spoon, remove the cooked pieces of fish and let cool.
- Remove bouquet garni and purée the soup in a hand-cranked food mill—this acts as a thickener.
- Top each grilled bread slice with lobster mousse. Using your fingers, shred the reserved cooked fish flesh and add to soup. Adjust seasonings.

NOTE:

During lobster season, replace lobster flesh with coral.

TIP

(1) To make coral butter, replace lobster meat with creamy coral that is found in raw or cooked lobster.

Poached Skate
with Lemon and Seaweed

4 servings · Difficulty: 2 · Preparation: 15 min · Cooking time: 15 min

- Heat court-bouillon and add white wine. The saucepan should be as large as possible. Eventually a broiling pan or jelly-roll pan will be used, as the skate slices take up a lot of space.

- Put the fish slices in the court-bouillon and simmer for approximately 10 to 12 minutes. To test for doneness, lift the flesh often. If it comes away easily from the bones, it is cooked. Turn off heat and keep slices in hot court-bouillon. This improves the flavor and helps tenderize the fish.

- Meanwhile, prepare the emulsion. In a blender or food processor, put lemon juice, egg yolks, and powdered seaweed[1]. While machine is on, incorporate little by little, the sunflower oil, which should be at room temperature (22°C or 72°F).

- Add parsley, salt and pepper. Set emulsion aside.

VEGETABLE ACCOMPANIMENT
Potatoes, boiled in salted water.

- 1 litre (4 cups) court-bouillon (see basic recipe pg. 12)
- 310 ml (1¼ cups) dry white wine
- 4 slices skate with skin, 210 g (7 oz) each, well washed
- Salt and pepper
- Juice of 2 lemons
- 2 egg yolks
- 15 g (½ oz) powdered seaweed
- 160 ml (⅔ cup) sunflower oil
- 5 ml (1 tsp) parsley or watercress, finely chopped
- Salt and pepper

SERVING SUGGESTION
With the help of a large spatula or slotted spoon, lift slices of skate[2] and place on a clean tea towel to absorb the liquid. Quickly remove skin, place on very hot plates, and pour 15 ml (1 tbsp) lemon emulsion over each serving.

TIP
(1) **Powdered seaweed:** Generally, the packaged seaweed that you buy can become damp from humidity. Place it in a 100°C (210°F) oven on paper towels until very dry. When dry, blend and powder by grinding in a coffee grinder. You can also purchase chopped or powdered seaweed.
(2) Leave the bones in cooked skate meat because it helps maintain its shape and prevents shrinkage.

GADIDAE—THE COD FAMILY

Gadoids are cold-water, cod-like fish. They are mostly found in the northern seas but some species are also established further south. They are in greater numbers in shallow water, although some also live in very deep waters.

Cod eat many other fish and invertebrates. This family has 59 species. Many species are of great commercial significance. Among all the fish families that we find here, the cod family is the largest, and the different varieties are well represented.

From a culinary point of view, all these fish have flaky flesh, allowing butter or sauce to slip in between the flakes when cooking.

Some fish in this group are well known around the world, especially cod. Others are not as well known and could provide an excellent substitute for cod, which is becoming scarce, because they are very flavorful and can be prepared in a number of ways.

Steamed Cod with Riced Potatoes and Grilled Pine Nuts

PREPARATION

- In a large saucepan, pour 1 litre (4 cups) water and 500 ml (2 cups) white wine. Add onion, carrots, bouquet garni, dried seaweed, peppercorns, and lemon juice. Cover and simmer gently for 20 minutes. Taste the court-bouillon and add salt if needed. Place a stainless steel steamer on the saucepan, making sure that the court-bouillon does not touch the bottom of the steamer. Salt and pepper each side of cod filets with sea salt and fresh ground white pepper. Cover and cook approximately 6 to 7 minutes, or until 70°C (160°F) is reached at thickest part of the filet.

RICED POTATOES AND GRILLED PINE NUTS

Creating an excellent potato purée is not as easy as it seems!

Choose potatoes that do not absorb liquid; it's better to cook the potatoes whole in salted water. They should be cooked well. While the potatoes are cooking, begin the following preparations:

- Heat cream or milk.
- Butter should be soft, at room temperature.
- Heat the potato ricer.
- Drain potatoes and press through the potato ricer. Do not use a food processor.
- Fold in the soft butter, followed by hot cream, salt and pepper to taste, and finally, add the grilled pine nuts.
- Serve immediately.

INGREDIENTS

- 500 ml (2 cups) white wine
- 1 small Spanish onion, finely sliced
- 1 medium carrot, finely sliced
- 1 bouquet garni
- 60 g (2 oz) dried seaweed
- 6 black peppercorns
- Juice of 1 lemon
- Sea salt
- Fresh ground pepper
- 4 cod filets 150 g to 180 g (5 oz to 6 oz) each, preferably thick

RICED POTATOES AND GRILLED PINE NUTS
- 1 kg (2.2 lbs) boiling potatoes (Idaho potatoes)
- 120 g (½ cup) soft, unsalted butter (room temperature)
- 180 ml (⅔ cup) 35% cream or milk
- Salt and fresh ground white pepper
- 90 g (¾ cup) grilled pine nuts

SERVING SUGGESTION (1st OPTION)
Pour the court-bouillon with added aromatics into a soup bowl, and place the cod filets in the center. Serve the riced potatoes and grilled pine nuts as a side dish.

SERVING SUGGESTION (2nd OPTION)
Serve the court-bouillon in a soup bowl along with the cooked vegetables. Serve the cod, riced potatoes and grilled pine nuts as an accompaniment on heated plates. As an added treat, top each filet with a dollop of room temperature butter.

Crêpes with Shredded Salt Cod and Capers

INGREDIENTS

CRÊPES (12)

- 115 g (³/₄ cup) stone ground flour[1] or white flour
- 40 g (¹/₄ cup) whole wheat or white flour
- 2 whole eggs
- Salt
- Sugar
- 125 ml (¹/₂ cup) water
- 160 ml (²/₃ cup) 3.25% milk
- 60 g (¹/₄ cup) soft butter

SHREDDED COD

- 390 g (13 oz) salt cod
- 500 ml (2 cups) court-bouillon (see recipe pg. 12)
- 625 ml (2¹/₂ cups) fish stock (see recipe pg. 12)
- 120 g (¹/₂ cup) capers
- Salt and pepper
- 180 g (³/₄ cup) soft unsalted butter (room temperature)
- 100 g (2¹/₂ cups) fresh bread crumbs

ALTERNATIVE FISH CHOICES

Any fish from the same family.

PREPARATION

CRÊPES

- In a stainless steel bowl, mix the flours, make a well in the center, and break in the whole eggs.

- Add a pinch of salt and sugar. Stir with a wooden spoon, incorporating the milk little by little until a smooth batter is obtained.

- Add the melted butter and refrigerate for 1 hour.

- Oil crêpe pan lightly with a paper towel.

- Stir crêpe batter once more, and using a small ladle, make 12 crêpes.

- Keep crêpes warm.

SHREDDED COD

- Soak salt cod for at least 6 hours, changing water frequently.
- Bring court-bouillon to a boil and cook the cod in it for 3 minutes. Drain and shred cod.
- Heat fish stock. Mix one half of stock with shredded cod and add capers. Adjust seasonings.
- Preheat oven to 200°C (400°F).
- Stuff crêpes with shredded cod mixture.
- Coat a baking dish generously with 60 g (¼ cup) butter; arrange crêpes in dish and nappe (cover) with the remaining fish stock. Sprinkle with white bread crumbs[2] and small chunks of remaining butter and bake for 15 minutes. Serve very hot.

INFORMATION

(1) Stone ground wheat flour can be replaced with buckwheat flour.

(2) White bread crumbs can be replaced with grated cheese, but this would mask the subtle sea flavors of cod.

Haddock Tian and Hazelnut Butter

4 Servings • Difficulty: 5 • Preparation: 30 min • Cooking time: 30 min

PARSNIP BASE

• In a skillet, heat butter and nut oil. Salt and pepper the parsnip slices and sear on medium until they begin to darken. Reduce heat, cover, and cook until tender when the tip of a knife is inserted. Parsnips keep their flavor better when they are not cooked in water.

• In a frying pan, heat butter and quickly cook spinach. Salt and pepper to taste and let cool.

TIAN

• In Provence, a tian is a shallow round earthenware dish in which gratins are made. Here, we use a stainless steel circular flan form 12 cm to 14 cm (4" to 5") in diameter.

• Place four stainless steel flan forms on a baking sheet or a broiling pan. Place two layers of parsnips in the bottom of each flan form, a layer of spinach, and end with two layers of parsnips. Keep hot in a 170°C (340°F) oven while the fish cooks.

• In a thick-bottomed skillet, heat butter and nut oil. Salt, pepper, and flour the haddock filets.

• Sauté until both sides are golden, reduce the heat, and coat with the butter mixture used to cook the fish. When the thickest part of the filets have reached 68°C (155°F) pour off the cooking oils and add 60 g (¼ cup) unsalted butter or hazelnut butter[1].

INFORMATION

(1) Hazelnut butter is found in health food stores.

PARSNIP BASE

- 60 g (¼ cup) unsalted butter
- 60 ml (¼ cup) hazelnut oil or nut oil of choice
- 400 g (4½ cups) medium parsnips, finely sliced
- Salt and fresh ground pepper
- 60 g (¼ cup) unsalted butter
- 300 g (6 cups) fresh spinach, well washed, drained, and stems removed

TIAN

- 60 g (¼ cup) unsalted butter
- 60 ml (⅓ cup) hazelnut oil or nut oil of choice
- 4 thick haddock filets
- Salt and fresh ground pepper
- 100 g (⅔ cup) sifted flour
- 60 g (¼ cup) soft unsalted butter or hazelnut butter (room temperature)
- Juice of 2 lemons

ALTERNATIVE FISH CHOICES

Any fish in the same family.

SERVING SUGGESTION

Using a spatula, place one layer of parsnip/spinach mixture on each heated plate and top with a haddock filet. Drizzle a little lemon juice and hazelnut butter on each filet. Serve very hot.

INGREDIENTS

BREAD CRUMBS
- Sliced white bread
- 120 g (¹/₂ cup) sun dried tomatoes
- 20 g (²/₃ cup) dried parsley

WHITING
- 2 egg yolks
- 60 ml (¹/₄ cup) milk
- Salt and fresh ground pepper
- 4 small whiting 210 g to 240 g (7 oz to 8 oz) each, well wiped and refrigerated
- 100 g (²/₃ cup) sifted flour
- 120 g (¹/₂ cup) unsalted butter
- 160 ml (²/₃ cup) veal broth or commercial equivalent

ALTERNATIVE FISH CHOICES
Any fish from the same family.

SERVING SUGGESTIONS
Pour very hot, thickened veal stock around each fish, and arrange small vegetables around fish.

PREPARATION

Ask your fishmonger to bone each whiting, keeping the tail and fins, or use the technique on page 69.

BREAD CRUMBS

• Leave bread 1 hour on counter to dry.

• Remove the crusts and place in bowl of food processor along with the sun dried tomatoes and parsley. Pulse until a fine crumb is obtained. The bread crumb mixture will keep several days refrigerated in an airtight container.

Whiting

• In a bowl, beat the egg yolks and milk.

• Salt and pepper the interior and exterior of whiting, flour, and dip in the yolk and milk mixture. Coat with the fresh bread crumb mixture.

• In a heavy-bottomed skillet heat butter and sear the whiting for 5 to 6 minutes, or until golden on each side, or until they are 68°C (155°F) in the thickest part. Reduce heat.

• Baste often as this fish is very delicate. The butter will be entirely absorbed by the whiting and will form a crust, keeping the interior moist.

Lobster and Shredded Cod
Puff Pockets

4 servings · Difficulty: 5 · Preparation: 35 min · Cooking time: 30 min

- Preheat oven to 200°C (400°F).

- Using a steamer, steam cod, covered, over salted water for approximately 10 minutes. When cooked, shred cod, salt and pepper, and refrigerate.

- Put the lobster bisque in a stainless steel bowl and incorporate the shredded cod. Adjust seasonings and refrigerate.

- Using a rolling pin, roll out puff pastry, cutting circles 18 cm (7") in diameter by 0.25 cm (1/16") thick.

- Using your thumb, press the circumference of each pastry circle and brush with egg yolk thinned with a little milk.

- Divide the lobster and cod mixture between the four pastry circles. Close one half of the circle over the other and thumb-press to seal. Brush surface with egg yolk and milk mixture.

- Using the tines of a fork, form a cross on the pastry and bake, making sure that the pastry is not too close to the bottom element, which could burn the bottom of the puff. When the puffs are cooked, place an upside down baking sheet over them for protection.

- Heat the lobster bisque.

- 300 g (10 oz) fresh cod
- 2 cans lobster paste, 200 g (approx. 7 oz) each[1]
- Salt and fresh ground pepper
- 600 g (20 oz) store-bought puff pastry
- 2 egg yolks
- 250 ml (1 cup) lobster bisque (see recipe pg. 15), or commercial equivalent
- 1 package leaf spinach

ALTERNATIVE FISH CHOICES
All fish of the same family.

SERVING SUGGESTION
Pour the sauce on the bottom of heated plates, top with a puff, and garnish with butter-sautéed spinach.

INFORMATION
(1) Canned lobster paste can be found at the fishmongers.

Cusk or Squirrel Hake Filets, Tomato Coulis, Capers and Mushrooms

- 60 ml (¼ cup) extra virgin olive oil
- 240 g (4 cups) firm white mushrooms, washed and diced
- 6 ripe tomatoes, cored, seeded, and diced
- 4 green onions, whites and green part, chopped
- 3 cloves garlic, crushed and finely diced
- 30 g (⅓ cup) carrots, finely diced
- 1 celery stalk, finely diced
- 175 ml (¾ cup) clam juice or fish stock (see recipe pg. 12)
- 1 bouquet garni
- Hot pepper
- Salt and pepper
- 4 large potatoes, sliced 3 mm (⅛") thick
- 4 hake or cusk filets 180 g (6 oz) each
- 60 g (¼ cup) capers
- 30 g (⅔ cup) chives, scissor cut

- In a skillet, heat olive oil. Sauté mushrooms until liquid evaporates, and add tomatoes, green onions, garlic, carrots, and celery. Sauté 3 to 4 minutes.
- Add clam juice, bouquet garni, and hot pepper. Salt and pepper to taste and set aside.
- Blanch potatoes in a saucepan of boiling water.
- Preheat oven to 180°C (350°F).
- In an oven-proof dish, place hake fillets side by side; salt and pepper.
- Pour half the tomato mushroom coulis over filets, sprinkle with capers, layer on sliced potatoes, and end with remaining coulis.
- Cover with wax paper or parchment paper and bake until the temperature of fish at thickest part is 68°C (155°F).
- Remove parchment paper, sprinkle with fresh chives, and serve very hot on a platter in the center of the table.

ALTERNATIVE FISH CHOICES
Any fish from the same family.

SALMONIDAE—THE SALMON FAMILY

For the cook, this is a noble family of fish. The beauty of salmon and their vivid color when cooked make for a festive meal.

The size of salmonids varies from medium to large. Their shape and appearance vary and they generally have a less compact shape than Atlantic herring.

Different names are given to salmon to distinguish their stages of development. The newly hatched are called alevins or sac fry. After the alevins emerge from the gravel bed and are less than one year old, they are called finger thick alevins. A little later they are called parr and stay 2 to 3 years in the stream where they were born. When they descend to the ocean for 2 to 3 years, they are called smolt, and are a bright silvery color. Those that return to fresh water after a winter at sea are called whitling, grilse, or peel. After spending 2 to 3 years at sea, the mature fish are called salmon. Salmon, like certain Arctic char, are anadromes—they live in salt water and reproduce in fresh water.

Fresh water salmon, also known as ouananiche, is generally smaller than the anadrome salmon. In the Atlantic there is only one species, Atlantic salmon, whereas in the Pacific, there are 5 species that are frequently caught.

Salmonidae – The Salmon Family

Small   Medium   Large

Maximum ★★★★; $$$$$
"Commonly Called" includes nicknames and misnomers

Arctic Grayling

Scientific name: *Thymallus arcticus* (Pallas, 1776). **Commonly called:** Blue fish, Arctic char. **Characteristics:** This fish is the grand prize of sport fishing but is becoming expensive, as it can only be fished in the great North. But what a fish! Very delicate, its flesh has thyme flavors. **Quality:** ★★★★★. **Sport fishing.**

Artic Char

Scientific name: *Salvelinus alpinus* (Linné, 1758). **Commonly called:** Arctic char. **Characteristics:** This fish can only be fished north of the 50th parallel. It has a very fine flesh, but does not take well to freezing. We find this farm-raised fish less "majestic" than wild ones. **Quality:** ★★★★. **Cost:** $$$$.

Lake Trout

Scientific name: *Salvelinus namaycush* (Walbaum, 1792). **Commonly called:** Grey trout. **Characteristics:** Lake Trout is a lake fish; it lives in deep water. Reaching an impressive weight, its flesh, when cooked, has a nutty flavor and melts in your mouth. **Quality:** ★★★★. **Cost:** $$$.

Brook Trout

Scientific name: *Salvelinus fontinalis* (Mitchill, 1814). **Commonly called:** Speckled trout. **Characteristics:** With a very fine flesh, brook trout is a highly valued sport fish. Its weight can reach 1.4 kg (3 lbs). **Quality:** ★★★★. **Cost:** $$$$.

Rainbow Trout

Scientific name: *Salmo gairdneri* (Richardson, 1836). **Commonly called:** Silver trout, Lake trout. **Characteristics:** This fish is the first salmonid to be raised on a fish farm. It has been devalued, but modern fish farms have greatly improved the quality of this trout. **Quality:** ★★★★. **Cost:** $$$.

Atlantic Salmon

Scientific name: *Salmo salar* (Linné, 1758). **Commonly called:** Landlocked salmon. **Characteristics:** Its weight can be from 1.4 kg to 9.2 kg (3 lbs to 20 lbs), and is the only one of the salmon family to live in the Atlantic Ocean. Thanks to fish farming, this majestic fish has become affordable to us all. **Quality:** ★★★★. **Cost:** $$$.

Sockeye Salmon

Scientific name: *Oncorhynchus nerka* (Walbaum, 1792). **Commonly called:** Red salmon. **Characteristics:** The best salmon of the large family of Pacific salmons. All Pacific salmons (male and female) die upon their return to fresh water after breeding; this is not the case with Atlantic salmon. **Quality:** ★★★★. **Cost:** $$$$.

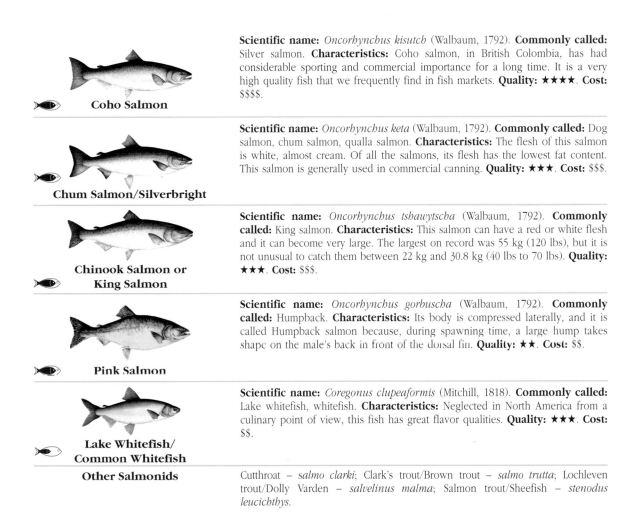

Coho Salmon

Scientific name: *Oncorhynchus kisutch* (Walbaum, 1792). **Commonly called:** Silver salmon. **Characteristics:** Coho salmon, in British Colombia, has had considerable sporting and commercial importance for a long time. It is a very high quality fish that we frequently find in fish markets. **Quality:** ★★★. **Cost:** $$$$.

Chum Salmon/Silverbright

Scientific name: *Oncorhynchus keta* (Walbaum, 1792). **Commonly called:** Dog salmon, chum salmon, qualla salmon. **Characteristics:** The flesh of this salmon is white, almost cream. Of all the salmons, its flesh has the lowest fat content. This salmon is generally used in commercial canning. **Quality:** ★★★. **Cost:** $$$.

Chinook Salmon or King Salmon

Scientific name: *Oncorhynchus tshawytscha* (Walbaum, 1792). **Commonly called:** King salmon. **Characteristics:** This salmon can have a red or white flesh and it can become very large. The largest on record was 55 kg (120 lbs), but it is not unusual to catch them between 22 kg and 30.8 kg (40 lbs to 70 lbs). **Quality:** ★★★. **Cost:** $$$.

Pink Salmon

Scientific name: *Oncorhynchus gorbuscha* (Walbaum, 1792). **Commonly called:** Humpback. **Characteristics:** Its body is compressed laterally, and it is called Humpback salmon because, during spawning time, a large hump takes shape on the male's back in front of the dorsal fin. **Quality:** ★★. **Cost:** $$.

Lake Whitefish/ Common Whitefish

Scientific name: *Coregonus clupeaformis* (Mitchill, 1818). **Commonly called:** Lake whitefish, whitefish. **Characteristics:** Neglected in North America from a culinary point of view, this fish has great flavor qualities. **Quality:** ★★★. **Cost:** $$.

Other Salmonids

Cutthroat – *salmo clarki*; Clark's trout/Brown trout – *salmo trutta*; Lochleven trout/Dolly Varden – *salvelinus malma*; Salmon trout/Sheefish – *stenodus leucichthys*.

Grilled Atlantic Salmon
in Red Wine Sauce

PREPARATION

INGREDIENTS

• Place shallots in a sauce pan, pour in red wine and reduce by 80%. Add fish stock and cook 3 to 4 minutes. Thicken slightly with a little white roux. Salt and pepper. While this is cooking, prepare toppings.

• Wash and wipe the chanterelle mushrooms well, halve if they are large. In a thick-bottomed skillet, heat butter, add chanterelles, and sauté on high. Add escargots, salt and pepper. Set aside. Oil, salt and pepper salmon slices and grill until they reach 65°C (150°F) at the thickest part.

- 3 shallots, chopped
- 750 ml (3 cups) robust red wine
- 250 ml (1 cup) fish stock (see recipe pg. 12)
- Salt and fresh ground pepper
- Cooked white roux (see recipe pg. 12)
- 80 g (⅓ cup) unsalted butter
- 400 g (6 ½ cups) chanterelle or wild mushrooms, slivered
- 24 canned Burgundy escargots, drained
- Salt and fresh ground pepper
- 20 ml (4 tsp) sunflower oil
- 4 salmon slices, 180 g (6 oz) each

ALTERNATIVE FISH CHOICES

Any fish in the salmon family, including whitefish.

SERVING SUGGESTION

Scatter chanterelle mushrooms and escargots on heated plates and nappe (cover) with red wine sauce.

TECHNIQUE

How to fillet a salmon:

| Slice along dorsal fins with knife. | Remove from bones. | Remove skin. | Cut filets into serving portions. |

Stuffed Arctic Char
with Fernand Point's Port Sauce

4 servings · Difficulty: 6 · Preparation: 40 min
· Cooking time: by thermometer

Ask your fishmonger to remove Arctic char bones, keeping the head and tail, or use technique shown on page 69.

• Open the fish, salt and pepper, wrap and refrigerate.

STUFFING

• In a skillet or saucepan, heat butter on medium low, add vegetables, salt and pepper, and stew gently until vegetables are cooked.

• Let cool and incorporate egg yolks.

• Preheat oven to 180°C (350°F).

• Open prepared Arctic char and spread the vegetables the length of the opening.

• Using a pastry brush, coat the edges with egg white. Close and place fish in an oven-proof dish.

• Sprinkle shallots on fish and pour port on top. Salt and pepper. Cover with buttered parchment paper and bake until fish reaches 68°C (155°F).

• Using a spatula, remove char, remove skin, and keep hot, covered with a damp tea towel.

• Reduce the cooking juices by 90%, and add thickened chicken stock and fish stock. Simmer a few minutes and strain. Adjust seasonings.

• 1 Arctic char 0.8 kg to 1 kg (1 ¾ lbs to 2 lbs)
• Salt and fresh ground pepper
• 80 g (⅓ cup) unsalted butter
• 1 small carrot, very finely sliced
• 2 stalks celery heart, very finely sliced
• 1 leek, white part, very finely sliced
• 1 parsnip, very finely sliced
• 100 g (2 cups) leaf spinach, very finely sliced
• 2 egg yolks, beaten
• 2 egg whites, beaten
• 310 ml (1 ¼ cups) port
• 60 g (⅓ cup) shallots, very finely chopped
• 15 ml (1 tbsp) unsalted butter
• 1 sheet aluminum foil or parchment paper
• 160 ml (⅔ cup) thickened chicken stock (see recipe pg. 17)
• 160 ml (⅔ cup) fish stock (see recipe pg. 12)
• 375 g (1 ½ cups) Parisian potatoes (potato balls using a melon scoop)

ALTERNATIVE FISH CHOICES

Any fish in the salmon family.

SERVING SUGGESTION

Place the Arctic char on a heated platter. Nappe (cover) with sauce and surround with potato balls that have been boiled in salted water.

REFLECTIONS

We've named this dish in honor of Mr. Fernand Point, one of the greatest chefs of the twentieth century. Arctic char is certainly one of the best fish found on our continent. However, there is one drawback! Arctic char is not a commercial fish and freezes poorly. Therefore, we have to use fish farm char, which, in spite of the good intentions of its producers, does not equal the flavor of a wild Arctic char. If you fish, drop a line above the 55th parallel in Canada or in the high mountain lakes of Europe.

Whitefish Papillote
with Vegetables and Herbs

4 servings · Difficulty: 4 · Preparation: 30 min
· Cooking time: approx. 15 min. per 500 g (1 lb)

- 1 whitefish, weighing 1 kg to 1.2 kg (2 ¼ lbs to 2 ½ lbs)
- Salt and fresh ground pepper
- 60 g (²/₃ cup) carrots, finely sliced
- ½ leek, white part, finely sliced
- 1 small parsnip, finely sliced
- 50 g (1 cup) spinach leaves, finely sliced
- 25 g (½ cup) chives, finely sliced
- 30 g (1 cup) lovage, coarsely chopped
- 20 g (²/₃ cup) parsley, coarsely chopped
- 25 g (1 cup) sorrel leaves, coarsely chopped
- Salt and fresh ground pepper
- ½ egg white
- 60 g (¼ cup) soft unsalted butter (room temperature)
- 160 ml (²/₃ cup) dry white wine
- 315 g (1 ¼ cups) bite-sized potatoes

SERVING SUGGESTION

Serve immediately with sautéed, baked, or potatoes boiled in salted water.

NOTE:

Do not remove the skin but scale the fish thoroughly. The skin of fish is edible. It protects the flesh and keeps it moist.

To "papillote" any food, in this case fish, you braise it in parchment paper that is folded to form a sealed packet. It is especially practical on the barbeque in the summer with fresh-caught fish. Use parchment paper or aluminum foil. Foil is practical to use but parchment paper is a healthier choice.

Whitefish, which we do not eat very much of in North America, is a prized fish in Europe, where it may be called lavarel (Savoy region of France) or féra. Both belong to the whitefish family.

- Remove fish bones on the belly side, being careful to remove every one. Keep the head and tail intact.

- Salt with sea salt and grind fresh black pepper on fish. Refrigerate in a clean dampened tea towel.

- In a saucepan filled with salted boiling water, cook carrots, leeks and parsnips until tender. Drain well.

- Thoroughly mix together the spinach, chives, lovage, parsley, and sorrel with the cooked vegetables. Add salt and pepper to mixture and fold in the lightly beaten egg whites.

- Spread out parchment paper or aluminum foil. Make it large enough to form edges to seal in the fish.

- Using a pastry brush, butter parchment paper well. Place open fish in the center, then spread herb and vegetable mixture in the center of the fish. Fold the fish over the filling; close the parchment paper, making several folds to form a seal on top. Leave one section open, pour in wine and complete closing and sealing so that the contents are airtight in the packet.

- Cook on the barbeque on medium heat or in the oven at 180°C (350°F). Count 15 minutes per 500 g (1 lb) of fish. This is an approximate time since you don't open the packet to check.

- When done, place the whitefish on a large heated platter in the center of the table, and with a knife or scissors, slice or cut open the papillote … What a wonderful aroma!

Brook Trout Amandine

4 servings · Difficulty: 3 · Preparation: 10 min · Cooking time: 10 min

This simple recipe, prepared with high quality ingredients, is a delicacy.

- Heat skillet with oil and 30 g (1 oz) butter.

- Season and flour the trout and place in pan when oil and butter mix is bubbling. Brown each side.

- Keep hot.

- Degrease pan and toast the almonds.

- Add remaining butter; heat until it turns a nutty brown (shortly after it bubbles).

- Pour lemon juice over trout, and then the browned butter and toasted almonds. The lemon juice will cause the butter to bubble once again on the trout.

INGREDIENTS

- 50 ml (¼ cup) oil
- 60 g (¼ cup) unsalted butter
- Flour
- 8 brook trout
- 30 g (1 oz) slivered almonds
- Salt and pepper
- Juice of 1 ½ lemons

SERVING SUGGESTION
Serve with a garden salad and fresh herbs.

Trout Flan with Crayfish Coulis

4 servings · Difficulty: 4 · Preparation: 40 min · Cooking time: 15 min

- Salt and pepper diced trout and refrigerate.

- Bring the milk and almond oil to a boil. Salt and pepper to taste.

- Put the diced trout into the boiling mixture and, when it returns to the boil, remove the diced fish with a slotted spoon and drain on paper towels.

- Reduce milk mixture by half.

- Incorporate cream and eggs. Adjust seasonings if necessary.

- Using a pastry brush, butter ramekins.

- Divide the diced trout evenly in ramekins and pour milk mixture over fish.

- Place ramekins in a pan with water halfway up ramekins at 130°C (270°F), and leave until the flans are firm.

- Sea salt and ground white pepper
- 480 g (1 lb) skinned trout filets, diced 0.5 cm x 0.5 cm (¼" x ¼")
- 500 ml (2 cups) milk
- 20 ml (4 tsp) almond oil
- 175 ml (¾ cup) 35% cream, very cold
- 4 eggs, lightly beaten
- 60 g (¼ cup) soft butter (room temperature)
- 175 ml (¾ cup) crayfish or lobster coulis (see recipe pg. 15)

SERVING SUGGESTION
Serve immediately, topping ramekins with 30 ml (2 tbsp) coulis.

Grilled Sockeye Salmon
with Lentils and Hazelnut Butter

INGREDIENTS

- 4 slices sockeye salmon 150 g to 180 g (5 oz to 6 oz) each
- Sea salt or sel de Guérande
- 100 g (1 cup) hazelnuts (filberts)
- 180 g (³/₄ cup) soft unsalted butter (room temperature)
- Juice of 1 lemon
- 15 g (¹/₂ cup) chervil, finely chopped
- Salt and ground white pepper
- 30 ml (2 tbsp) sunflower oil

LENTILS

- 250 g (1 ¹/₃ cups) du Puy[1] lentils or red lentils
- ¹/₂ onion
- ¹/₂ carrot
- ¹/₂ stalk celery
- 1 bay leaf
- 6 peppercorns
- 2 garlic cloves in skin
- Sea salt

SERVING SUGGESTION

Place salmon on very hot dinner plates, arrange lentils to side and let the guests help themselves to the hazelnut butter.

INFORMATION

(1) The "du Puy" is the quality control mark of one of the very best lentils available, but you may use any lentil of your choice.

PREPARATION

- Dry salmon slices well, sprinkle with a little sea salt (sel de Guérande, France) and refrigerate.

HAZELNUT OR FILBERT BUTTER

- If you buy filberts with skins on, they must be removed by boiling in 500 ml (2 cups) water for 1 minute.
- Run under cold water, remove the skins, and dry well.
- Grind as fine as possible, stir in butter, add lemon juice and chervil. Salt and pepper. Keep at room temperature.

LENTILS

- Generally, lentils do not need to be pre-soaked for several hours.
- In a saucepan containing 2 litres (8 cups) of water, boil the onion, carrots, celery, bay leaf, pepper, and garlic for 20 minutes.
- Add lentils and cook until they are cooked but still firm.
- Salt, drain, and keep hot.
- In this recipe, the hazelnut (filbert) butter will lighten the flavor.

SALMON

- Proceed with steps to grill fish as follows:
- Coat fish with oil using a pastry brush.
- Grill both sides, turning to form square grill marks, on high heat.
- Reduce heat to medium.
- Reduce to low and cook salmon to 68°C (155°F) at its thickest part.
- Always place fish to the side of the grill to rest for a few minutes when done.

Brook Trout and Scallop Turbans with Vanilla White Butter

4 servings · Difficulty: 5 · Preparation: 30 min · Cooking time: 20 min

SOCKEYE SALMON FILETS

• Using the flat blade of a large knife, gently flatten the filets until large enough to contain the scallop mousse. Set aside.

SCALLOP MOUSSE

• Wipe the scallops well and place in food processor. Add salt and pepper. Blend 30 seconds; add egg white and cream. Refrigerate 30 minutes.

• Preheat oven to 155°C (310°F).

ASSEMBLY

• Butter ramekins well using a pastry brush.

• Salt and pepper brook trout on each side and flatten against inside edges of ramekins. Fill centers with scallop mousse.

• Cover each ramekin with plastic wrap and refrigerate for 1 hour.

• Pour 1 litre (4 cups) water in a large jellyroll pan or broiling pan. Arrange ramekins in pan and bake until they reach 68°C (155°F) in the center. During baking, prepare vanilla white butter.

• Also during baking, cook spinach as follows:

• In a heavy-bottomed skillet, heat butter and sauté until liquid evaporates.

• Grilled scallops may be added.

INGREDIENTS

- 4 small trout filets
- Salt and ground white pepper
- 300 g (10 oz) scallops
- 1/2 egg white
- 160 ml (2/3 cup) 35% cream
- 60 g (1/4 cup) soft, unsalted butter
- 310 ml (1 1/4 cups) white butter (see recipe pg. 13)[1]
- 1/2 drop of vanilla
- 500 g (10 cups) spinach leaves
- 60 g (1/4 cup) soft, unsalted butter (room temperature)
- Salt and fresh ground pepper

ALTERNATIVE FISH CHOICES

Any fish in the salmon family.

SERVING SUGGESTION

Coat the bottom of hot dinner plate with spinach and place ramekin in center. Serve immediately with vanilla white butter in a separate sauce dish.

TIP

[1] It is important to make the white butter at the last minute since it is very fragile and must be served immediately as soon as it is cooked. A half drop of vanilla complements the flavor of the fish.

WHY ADD VANILLA?

Brook trout is a very delicate fish with a slight nutty flavor. Just a tiny bit of vanilla highlights the flavor.

Rainbow Trout and Almond Mousse
with Mayonnaise

4 servings · Difficulty: 6 · Preparation: 40 min · Cooking time: 20 to 30 min

STUFFING

- Grind almonds in food processor until very fine. Reserve in a bowl.

- Put parsley and trout filets in bowl of food processor. Blend and add salt and pepper. Incorporate egg white and cream, add ground almonds, and set aside.

- Debone trout belly. Salt and pepper.

- Preheat oven to 200°C (400°F).

- Divide and spread stuffing between the opened trout. Close fish one side over the other and place in an oven-proof dish.

- Pour fish stock over trout. Cover with parchment paper and bake until 68°C (155°F) is reached at the thickest part.

- Remove skin from hot baked fish, place fish in cooking juices, and refrigerate overnight.

EGGS MIMOSA

- In a saucepan of boiling water, cook eggs until hard, 8 to 10 minutes, depending upon size of eggs. When cooked, place under cold running water. Shell and cut lengthwise.

- Remove the yolks and rub through a sieve. Add half the mayonnaise, mix well, and add salt and pepper. Keep the rest of the mayonnaise for the stuffed tomatoes. Refill the halved eggs with mixture. Decorate each egg with a small parsley leaf.

MACÉDOINE STUFFED TOMATOES

- Cut around the stem end and remove the stem plus some of interior of tomatoes in one piece, without damaging the skin. Salt and pepper interior and replace cut-out section.

- Cook diced vegetable mix in salted boiling water. Drain and place under running cold water. Drain well. Press to extract the remaining water. Salt and pepper. Add 80 g (⅓ cup) of the remaining mayonnaise, mix well, and stuff cavity of tomatoes with the macédoine of vegetables.

INGREDIENTS

- 100 g (1 cup) almonds, peeled
- 40 g (1 ⅓ cups) parsley, stems removed, washed, drained, and dried
- 120 g (4 oz) trout filets (approx. 3)
- Sea salt and ground white pepper
- 1 egg white
- 60 ml (¼ cup) 35% very cold cream
- 4 rainbow trout, 160 g to 180 g (5 oz to 6 oz) each
- 250 ml (1 cup) light fish stock (see recipe pg. 12)
- 200 g (¾ cup) of mayonnaise

GARNITURE

- 4 eggs
- 160 g (⅔ cup) mayonnaise
- 4 small tomatoes
- 300 g (3 ⅓ cups) macédoine of vegetables, frozen or fresh (mixed diced vegetables)

ALTERNATIVE FISH CHOICES

Any small fish 150 g to 210 g (5 oz to 7 oz) in the salmon family.

SERVING SUGGESTION

Thirty minutes before serving, drain fish and carefully wipe off any cooking juices. Thin 200 g (¾ cup) mayonnaise with a little water so that it will nappe (cover) the fish well. Place a cooked fish on each plate, nappe with thinned mayonnaise, and decorate with Eggs Mimosa and Macédoine Stuffed Tomatoes.

Salmon and Halibut Mousse
with Yoghurt Sauce

INGREDIENTS

SALMON MOUSSE
- 150 g (5 oz) salmon
- 1 egg
- 80 ml (⅓ cup) 35% cream
- Salt and ground white pepper

HALIBUT MOUSSE
- 150 g (5 oz) halibut
- 1 egg
- 80 ml (⅓ cup) 35% very cold cream
- Salt and ground white pepper

YOGHURT SAUCE
- 90 g (⅓ cup) plain yoghurt
- 80 ml (⅓ cup) sour cream
- 15 g (⅓ cup) chives, scissor cut
- 30 g (⅛ cup) dried tomatoes, small dice
- Salt and ground white pepper
- Finely sliced baguette, grilled

ALTERNATIVE FISH CHOICES
Any fish without a pronounced flavor.

SERVING SUGGESTION
Serve one jar of mousse per guest accompanied by grilled baguette and Yoghurt Sauce.

PREPARATION

This is a lovely summer main course: for it, you need 8 one-half-cup preserving jars.

SALMON MOUSSE
- Finely chop salmon by pulsing in a food processor and set aside.
- Whisk egg in a bowl until well blended. Add cream, salt and pepper.
- Gently fold in the salmon, pour mixture into the small preserving jars, and refrigerate one hour.

HALIBUT MOUSSE: REPEAT ABOVE METHOD USING HALIBUT.
- Preheat oven to 200°C (400°F).
- Place jars in oven broiler or large oven-proof pan. Add water to bottom of pan and cook until 70°C (160°F) is reached at the center of the jar. Cool.
- The potted mousse can be refrigerated several days.

YOGHURT SAUCE
- In a bowl, mix yoghurt and sour cream, add chives and dried tomatoes. Salt and pepper to taste.

TECHNIQUE
How to debone a fish (in this case, a trout) from the belly before stuffing:

Slide the knife under the bones of one side, and then the other.　　Remove the center bone.

Sautéed Lake Trout with Pistachio Coulis

INGREDIENTS

- 150 g (1 ½ cups) pistachios, skin removed
- 175 ml (¾ cup) milk
- 160 ml (⅔ cup) reduced fish stock (see recipe pg. 12)
- 80 g (⅓ cup) soft unsalted butter (room temperature)
- Juice of ½ lemon
- Salt and ground white pepper
- 4 lake trout 150 g (5 oz) each (large fish)
- Salt and ground white pepper
- Sifted flour
- 60 ml (¼ cup) cooking oil
- 60 g (¼ cup) unsalted butter

ALTERNATIVE FISH CHOICES

Any fish in the salmon family.

SERVING SUGGESTION

Place vegetables of choice in center of plate, top with trout filet, and garnish with pistachio coulis.

PREPARATION

PISTACHIO COULIS

- Using a food processor or coffee grinder, finely grind the pistachio nuts.
- In a saucepan, heat milk, add ground pistachios, and leave it to infuse 12 minutes.
- Add reduced fish stock and simmer 12 more minutes.
- Pour mixture into bowl of food processor or standing electric mixer and blend until it emulsifies while slowly adding soft butter and lemon juice.
- Add seasonings and keep warm.

PREPARING FISH

- Carefully wipe trout filets. Salt, pepper, and flour.
- In a heavy-bottomed skillet, heat butter and oil, and sear each side of filets until golden.
- Reduce heat and cook until 68°C (155°F) is reached at thickest part. Place filets to one side of skillet and keep warm.

VEGETABLE SUGGESTIONS

- Prepare sautéed mushrooms, spinach in butter, mashed potatoes, or seasonal vegetables.

SCOMBRIDAE FAMILY

These fish are very important commercially. We will not deal with them all in this chapter, but it is important that they be mentioned: King mackerel, Atlantic mackerel, white mackerel, Atlantic bonito, blue fin tuna, albacore tuna, and yellowfin tuna. In general, the same species are available in Europe.

Scombridae inhabit the deepest parts of the sea, and are great swimmers. Their bodies are slender and they are easily recognizable by the characteristic shape of their tail, which has a deeply cut-out fin. Between the dorsal and caudal fins there are several types of small lobes, which are also found between the anal fin and the caudal fin.

CLUPEIDAE FAMILY

These bony fish are the largest and most numerous in this category. The caudal fin has two lobes, the skeleton is made of bony tissue, and the vertebrae are well developed. The scales are shaped like small bony platelets. These are relatively primitive fish that live mostly in the deepest parts of the sea. Their bladder is connected to their digestive tube. The Clupeidae comprise of about 20 families. They live in shoals and feed on plankton.

Scombridae and Clupeidae
– The Mackerel, Tuna, Bonito and Herring Families

 Small  Medium  Large

Maximum ★★★★; $$$$$
"Commonly Called" includes nicknames and misnomers

Bluefin Tuna

Scientific name: *Thunnus thynnus* (Linné, 1758). **Characteristics:** Bluefin tuna can reach 900 kg to 1,000 kg (1,980 lbs to 2,200 lbs). Its back is dark blue; its belly is grey with silver marks; its dorsal fins are dark; and its anal fins are silver grey. **Quality:** ★★★★★. **Cost:** $$$$$.

Yellowfin Tuna

Scientific name: *Thunnus albacares* (Bonnaterre, 1788). **Commonly called:** Allison's tuna, tunny. **Characteristics:** A little thinner than bluefin tuna, the yellow color of its second dorsal fin from anal to caudal differentiates it from other tunas. It can reach 1.75 m (5'9") and weigh 135 kg (300 lbs). **Quality:** ★★★. **Cost:** $$$.

Albacore Tuna

Scientific name: *Thunnus alalunga* (Bonnaterre, 1788). **Commonly called:** Albacore, tuna, taupe. **Characteristics:** The back and sides of the albacore tuna are metallic blue, and its belly is silver. It stands out among other tunas and Scombridae by its very long pectoral fins. It can reach 120 cm (45") and weigh 34 kg to 36 kg (75 lbs to 80 lbs). **Quality:** ★★★. **Cost:** $$.

Atlantic Bonito

Scientific name: *Sarda sarda* (Bloch, 1793). **Commonly called:** Bonita, bonito. **Characteristics:** The Atlantic bonito has a metallic steel-blue back with silver flanks. It has seven lines of dark blue coloring going down to the base of the front part. It can reach 120 cm (47"), and its weight varies from 4 kg to 10 kg (8 lbs to 22 lbs). **Quality:** ★★★. **Cost:** $$$.

Atlantic Mackerel

Scientific name: *Scomber scombrus* (Linné, 1758). **Commonly called:** Blue fish, Lisette. **Characteristics:** It is small—50 g to 100 g (2 oz to3 oz). Its color of dark steel-blue with 23 to 33 wavy and dark stripes makes it rather pleasant to watch and touch. Its weight can reach 2 kg (4½ lbs), but its ideal weight for cooking is 300 g to 400 g (10 to 14 oz). **Quality:** ★★★★. **Cost:** $.

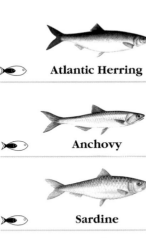

Atlantic Herring

Scientific name: *Clupea harengus harengus* (Linné, 1758). **Commonly called:** Sardine. **Characteristics:** Very popular in North America, it has a bright bluish tinge on its belly, with eyes surrounded by a reddish color. Its average length is 50 cm (20") with a weight of 600 g (20 oz). **Quality: ★★★. Cost: $.**

Anchovy

Scientific name: *Engraulis encrasicolus* (Linné, 1758). **Commonly called:** Pilchard, sardine. **Characteristics:** Used most often in filets and preserved, this small fish, when fresh, is very delicate. Its eyes are larger than that of the sardine. **Quality: ★★★. Cost: $$.**

Sardine

Scientific name: *Sardina pilchardus* (Walbaum, 1792). **Commonly called:** Pilchard, anchovy, herring. **Characteristics:** This little silver-blue fish has a series of small black marks behind its striped operculum. Its large scales can be easily removed. **Quality: ★★★★. Cost: $.**

Alewife

Scientific name: *Alosa pseudoharengus* (Wilson, 1811). **Commonly called:** Herring. **Characteristics:** This fish is an anadrome. It spawns in lakes, then returns to the sea. Its back of greyish green color has silver flanks. Its average weight is from 240 g (8 oz) to 300 g (10 oz). **Quality: ★★. Cost: $.**

Other Fish from the Same Families

Frigate Mackerel – *Auxis thazard* (Lacépède, 1802); Skipjack Tuna – *Euthynnus Pelamis* (Linné, 1758); Chub Mackerel – *Scomber colias* (Gmelin, 1789); Bigeye Tuna – *Thunnus obesus* (Lowe, 1839); Listao – *Katsuwonus pelamis*; Chub Mackerel – *Scomber colias* (Gmelin, 1789).

Mackerel Filets in White Wine

4 servings · Difficulty: 3 · Preparation: 20 min · Cooking time: 12 to 15 min

- Heat court-bouillon. Add lemons, white wine, coriander seed, and peppercorns. Cook approximately 7 to 8 minutes and keep warm.

- Wipe mackerel filets well, sprinkle with salt and refrigerate.

- Preheat oven to 195°C (380°F).

- Place mackerel filets side by side in an oven-proof baking dish with skin side up. Pour on hot court-bouillon, cover and bake 7 to 8 minutes. Refrigerate filets at least 24 hours to develop the flavor.

- 500 ml (2 cups) court-bouillon (see recipe pg. 12)
- 2 peeled lemons, sliced
- 175 ml (³/₄ cup) dry white wine
- 5 ml (1 tsp) coriander seed[1]
- 10 black peppercorns
- 8 mackerel filets 90 g to 120 g (3 oz to 4 oz) each
- Sea salt

ALTERNATIVE FISH CHOICES

Shad filets, Chub mackerel filets.

SERVING SUGGESTION

Place 2 mackerel filets on a chilled plate, nappe (cover) with jellied court-bouillon along with the vegetables cooked in court-bouillon. A green salad is a good accompaniment for this summer main course.

INFORMATION

(1) **Coriander:** This is a herb that originates from the Middle East and measures 20 cm to 80 cm. It is valued for its fruity aroma and delicate spicy taste. The leaves are used fresh and the seed dried.

Atlantic Bonito
with Tomatoes and Black Olives

4 servings · Difficulty: 3 · Preparation: 20 min
· Cooking time: by thermometer

- 2 cans peeled tomatoes, 390 ml (14 oz), or fresh tomatoes
- 60 ml (¼ cup) extra virgin olive oil
- 90 g (1 cup) onions, large dice
- 3 cloves garlic, finely chopped
- 5 g (¼ cup) herbes de Provence[1]
- 310 ml (1 ¼ cups) fish stock (see recipe pg. 12)
- Sea salt and fresh ground pepper
- 4 thick pieces Atlantic bonito 80 g (6 oz) each
- 60 ml (¼ cup) olive oil
- 24 black olives, pitted
- 20 g (⅔ cup) chopped parsley

- Drain tomatoes and press to extract the maximum amount of juice. Crush with a knife and set aside. Keep the juice for another recipe.

- In a thick-bottomed saucepan, heat oil and sear onions and garlic. Add tomatoes, herbes de Provence, fish stock, salt and pepper, and cook for 20 minutes.

- Salt and pepper the fish pieces.

- In a skillet, heat the oil, sear the fish pieces on each side, and place in an oven-proof baking dish. Cover completely with the tomato mixture and black olives.

- Cover and bake until fish reaches 68°C (155°F) at thickest part.

ALTERNATIVE FISH CHOICES
Tuna, albacore tuna, alewife.

SERVING SUGGESTION
This makes a great hot main course or a cold one on a hot day.

INFORMATION
(1) Herbes de Provence originated in Provence, France, and consists of thyme, bay leaf, savory, rosemary, tarragon, marjoram, and basil.

SERVING SUGGESTION
Cold: Serve cold, covered with tomato and olive mixture, accompanied with bite-sized cold potatoes.
Hot: Cover bottom of dinner plate with hot fried potatoes, place fish piece in center, and top with tomato mixture. Sprinkle with chopped parsley.

Turmeric Mackerel with Coconut Milk and Water Chestnuts

4 servings · Difficulty: 5 · Preparation: 25 min · Cooking time: 15 min

To make this recipe the Indonesian way, a spiced paste must be prepared first.

- In a blender or food processor, mix hot peppers, garlic, shallots, turmeric, ginger, whole cloves, coriander seed, dried shrimp paste, and lemon grass to make a paste.

- In a small saucepan, heat oil and cook spice mixture on low for 5 minutes. Cool.

- Heat fish stock; add coconut milk and cooled spiced paste. Cook 20 minutes.

- Add pulp of the tamarind and rub through a strainer.

- Cook mackerel in a salted court-bouillon with water chestnuts and peas until it reaches 64°C (150°F) at its thickest part.

INGREDIENTS

- 5 red hot peppers, seeded
- 3 cloves garlic, finely chopped
- 7 shallots, finely chopped
- 30 ml (2 tbsp) fresh or powdered turmeric
- 25 g (¼ cup) ginger, peeled and chopped
- 1 whole clove
- 15 ml (1 tbsp) coriander seed
- 30 g (1 oz) shrimp paste
- 1 cinnamon stick, chopped
- 60 ml (¼ cup) extra virgin olive oil
- 375 ml (1 ½ cups) fish stock, reduced (see recipe pg. 12)
- 375 ml (1 ½ cups) coconut milk
- 30 g (1 oz) tamarind pulp
- 4 mackerel filets 160 g to 180 g (6 oz) each
- Salt and pepper
- 360 g (2 cups) water chestnuts
- 50 g (½ cup) frozen or fresh peas

INFORMATION

Water chestnuts: This tuber originated in the Far East. Its crunchy white flesh reminds us of a fresh chestnut, a little sweeter but less starchy. Raw, boiled, or roasted, this vegetable is available fresh or canned.

INFORMATION

Turmeric: This is a bright yellow rhizome of the ginger family with a very pronounced flavor.
Tamarind: This is the fruit of the tamarind tree. The pods are filled with an acidic juicy pulp that gives a tart fruity flavor to food. Tamarind is sold in packages containing the pulp, seed, and fiber.

ALTERNATIVE FISH CHOICES

Tuna, herring, alewife, shad.

SERVING SUGGESTION

Serve mackerel, water chestnuts, and bouillon in soup plates. Accompany with white rice.

Grilled Tuna with Sauce Choron, and Crosne in Hazelnut Butter

4 servings • Difficulty: 3 • Preparation: 20 min • Cooking time: 10 min

- 400 g (2 ½ cups) crosnes, well washed
- 310 ml (1 ¼ cups) choron sauce
- 4 thick slices tuna 150 g to 180 g (5 oz to 6 oz) each
- Salt and fresh ground pepper
- 60 ml (¼ cup) olive oil
- 80 g (⅓ cup) hazelnut butter
- 30 g (1 cup) chervil leaves

- In a saucepan of salted boiling water, cook the crosnes until they are al dente. Run under cold water, drain, and set aside.

- Prepare choron sauce: see recipe for béarnaise sauce, pg. 14, to which tomato paste is added.

- Wipe tuna well; salt and pepper and brush with oil. Grill tuna following instructions (see pg. 92) until it reaches 68°C (155°F) at the thickest part.

- While tuna is cooking, gently heat the hazelnut butter in a frying pan and sauté the crosnes. Salt and pepper to taste.

ALTERNATIVE FISH CHOICES

Swordfish, mahi-mahi, blue marlin, shark, sturgeon.

SERVING SUGGESTIONS

Place tuna on individual heated plates and surround with crosnes. Sprinkle crosnes with chervil leaves. Choron sauce is always served separately.

INFORMATION

Crosnes, also known as Chinese artichokes, are a "forgotten vegetable" – they are small twirly tubers grown in Japan. An old and unusual variety, they have recently been rediscovered.

Grilled Sardines
with Saffron Lime Butter

INGREDIENTS

SAFFRON INFUSION
- Juice of 4 fresh limes
- A pinch of saffron, crushed

SARDINES
- 240 g (1 lb) unsalted butter, at room temperature
- 5 ml (1 tsp) fine salt
- 2 1/2 ml (1/2 tsp) fresh ground white pepper
- 800 g (1 3/4 lbs) small fresh sardines
- Salt and ground white pepper
- 60 ml (1/4 cup) olive oil
- 300 g (1/2 lb) small round potatoes

ALTERNATIVE FISH CHOICES

Anchovies, small perch, smelt, poor cod.

SERVING SUGGESTION

Place sardines on heated plates and nappe (cover) with lime saffron butter. Accompany with potatoes cooked in salted water.

PREPARATION

SAFFRON INFUSION

• In an airtight jar, mix lime juice and saffron and infuse overnight at room temperature. This procedure is very effective for developing the flavor of the saffron.

SARDINES

• Thirty minutes before preparing the sardines, add approximately 2½ ml (½ tsp) salt and 1 ml (¼ tsp) ground white pepper to Saffron Infusion. The acidity will dissolve the salt.

• After 30 minutes, add butter, and mix well until soft and smooth. Set aside.

• Heat both sides of the barbeque grill: one on high and the other on medium heat.

• Wipe sardines well; salt and pepper interior and exterior of sardines.

• Brush each lightly with oil and sear each side on high, turning to form square grill marks. Finish grilling on medium heat. Sardines are cooked when 65°C (150°F) is reached at the thickest part.

• Cook potatoes as an accompaniment in boiling salted water.

Smoked Herring in Oil with Warm Potatoes

4 servings · Difficulty: 3 · Preparation: 25 min

INGREDIENTS

- 1 kg (2.2 lbs) smoked herring
- 4 medium onions, finely sliced
- 3 carrots, finely sliced
- 6 cloves garlic, slivered
- 5 g (¼ cup) powdered celery
- 4 cloves
- 3 bay leaves
- 18 peppercorns
- 3 sprigs thyme
- Grapeseed or sunflower oil
- 4 medium potatoes
- Salt and fresh ground pepper

PREPARATION

This dish is usually served in winter. The great advantage is that it can be stored for 2 to 3 months.

NOTE: It is important to carefully choose smoked herring filets. There are two methods of smoking them; one is highly smoked, and the second method smokes them less and they remain soft. The latter is the best choice, but if you can't find lighter smoked herring, soak the former in milk for at least 24 hours, drain well, and wipe.

- In a large airtight container (preferably glass), put a layer of herring, a layer of mixed onions, carrots, garlic, celery powder, 1 clove, 1 bay leaf, 6 peppercorns and a sprig of thyme. Repeat the process two more times and cover with grape seed oil. Cover the container and store in cold room, cool basement, or refrigerate. The advantage of cool basement storage is that the flavor of the spices and herbs is better infused into the herring.

- Cook unpeeled potatoes in boiling salted water until tender. While still hot, peel potatoes and cut into 5 cm (¼") slices.

SERVING SUGGESTION

Place three hot potato slices on heated plates and top with herring. Sprinkle with salt and pepper. The heat of the potatoes will be sufficient to soften the herring filets.

NOTE:

It is important to transfer the herring filets with tongs or a slotted spoon to avoid including the marinade.

Tuna and Artichoke Wraps

4 servings · Difficulty: 4 · Preparation: 40 min · Cooking time: 20 min

- If fresh artichokes are used, cook in a large amount of boiling water. As soon as the center leaves pull out easily, stop cooking by running artichokes under cold water. Remove the leaves, which can be served separately with a vinaigrette, and keep the hearts, being sure to remove all of the fuzzy choke. Set aside.

- Salt and pepper the tuna.

- In a thick-bottomed skillet, heat oil and quickly sear both sides of tuna until golden. Set aside.

- Spread out caul fat. Salt and pepper.

- Evenly divide half of slivered artichoke heart between four cauls, top with tuna piece, and cover with remaining slivered artichoke heart. Form a packet using the caul fat around each fish piece.

- In a thick-bottomed skillet, heat butter and sear packets of artichoke and on high heat 2 to 3 minutes each side.

- Pour off fat, sprinkle with shallots. Pour in white wine, add lobster bisque, and simmer 3 to 4 minutes. Adjust seasonings.

- Cook the potatoes in boiling salted water.

- 4 medium fresh artichokes or 8 preserved hearts, slivered
- 4 tuna pieces 150 g to 180 g (5 oz to 6 oz) each
- Salt and fresh ground pepper
- 60 ml (¼ cup) peanut or other cooking oil
- 4 pieces of caul fat[1] 10 cm x 10 cm (4" x 4")
- 80 g (⅓ cup) unsalted butter
- 60 g (⅓ cup) shallots, finely chopped
- 125 ml (½ cup) white wine
- 175 ml (¾ cup) lobster bisque (see recipe pg. 15), or use commercially prepared
- 4 potatoes

ALTERNATIVE FISH CHOICES

Yellowfin tuna, tuna, Atlantic bonito, frigate mackerel, monk fish, shark.

SERVING SUGGESTION

Serve very hot in heated soup dishes, accompanied with potatoes cooked in salted water.

INFORMATION

(1) Caul fat is a lace-like fatty membrane taken from the abdominal cavities of pigs and sheep, and mostly used to wrap pâtés or dry meats, fish, etc.

DIVERSE FAMILIES

This group includes several families that usually are found in the more temperate waters of the south. They are all spiny fin fish except for the monk fish. Their general appearance and shape vary considerably, some species being very high and compact laterally, while others are spindle-shaped. The perciformes family, such as bass, perch, grouper, and red grouper, are part of a group that includes 80 different types worldwide. Others mostly live on the bottom or in the shallow waters of the warmer seas. With some, the head is enclosed in a bony case like an armor plate (gurnard, shorthorn, sculpin). Each has different flavor characteristics.

Grilled Sea Bass
with Almond Butter

4 servings · Difficulty: 2 · Preparation: 15 min · Cooking time: 20 min

When grilling a whole fish, it is essential to prepare the fish and the fish cage properly, whether it is on the barbecue or a stove grill. You could even cook this in a fireplace.

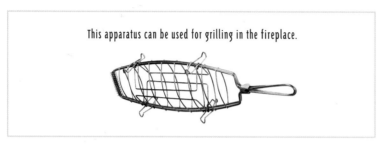

This apparatus can be used for grilling in the fireplace.

• Wipe sea bass well and wrap in a clean tea towel for several hours to remove all moisture.

• Brush sea bass with oil. Salt and pepper.

• Sear both sides of bass on section of grill on high, and then transfer them to medium heat section.

• Grill bass for the last 10 minutes of cooking time on low. It should be 68°C (155°F) at the thickest part.

• Never finish cooking a grilled fish in the oven. Grilling produces a crisp exterior and moist interior.

• While the bass is on the grill, prepare almond milk emulsion. Pour almond milk into the bowl of a standing electric mixer; add lime juice, salt, pepper, and the hot clarified butter while the machine is running.

INGREDIENTS

- 2 sea bass 600 g to 800 g (20 oz to 28 oz)
- 60 ml (¼ cup) sunflower oil
- Sea salt and fresh ground pepper
- 125 ml (½ cup) almond milk
- Juice of 2 limes
- 160 g (⅔ cup) clarified butter
- Salt and white pepper

ALTERNATIVE FISH CHOICES

Bluefish, white perch, grey weakfish, bluefish, swordfish, mahi-mahi.

SERVING SUGGESTION

Grilled fish does not wait! It must be served immediately with accompanying flavored butter. Small potatoes, plain or Parisienne style, or sautéed hazelnuts are a good accompaniment.

TECHNIQUE

Heat the grill on three temperatures.

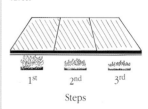

1st   2nd   3rd

Steps

INGREDIENTS

- 6 juicing oranges
- 60 g (¼ cup) unsalted butter
- 310 ml (1 ¼ cups) light fish stock (see recipe pg. 12)
- 5 g (¼ cup) saffron filaments
- Salt and fresh ground pepper
- 480 g (1 lb) bite-sized potatoes
- 4 tilefish filets or whites[1] (6 oz) each
- 15 g (½ cup) fresh parsley, chopped

ALTERNATIVE FISH CHOICES

Red grouper, monkfish, swordfish, tuna, mahi-mahi, shark.

PREPARATION

4 servings · Difficulty: 3 · Preparation: 30 min · Cooking time: 30 min

- Peel two oranges down to the flesh, removing all pith. With a very sharp knife, quarter and remove the membranes so that you end up only with flesh sections.

- In a thick-bottomed skillet, heat butter and sear each side of orange sections for 15 seconds. Keep warm.

- Juice 4 oranges, add fish stock, saffron, salt, and a pinch of pepper; heat and cook small potatoes in bouillon until tender.

- Remove potatoes from bouillon and keep warm.

- Reduce bouillon by half and add tilefish filets.

- Bake in a 90°C (190°F) oven until filets reach 68°C (155°F) at thickest part.

- Divide bouillon into heated soup dishes, top with tilefish filet, and surround with potatoes. Garnish with parsley and orange sections.

INFORMATION

(1) **Tilefish whites:** In modern cooking terminology, filets may be called whites.

Grape Leaf Wrapped
Goatfish in Lemon Butter

4 servings · Difficulty: 4 · Preparation: 20 min · Cooking time: 15 min

- Wash goatfish well, leaving head on. Wipe and refrigerate, wrapped in a clean tea towel or paper towel.

- Rinse grape leaves, leaving to soak in cold water for 1 hour. Dry on paper towel or clean tea towel.

- Heat exterior or interior grill on three temperatures (see grilling instructions pg. 27). Salt and pepper exterior and interior of goatfish and stuff with pistachios.

- Brush fish with cooking oil and sear on both sides until golden.

- Spread grape leaves on work surface, dust with powdered mushrooms. Remove fish from grill and wrap with leaves.

- Continue grilling on medium heat and complete cooking on low until 68°C (155°F) is reached at the thickest part.

- Meanwhile, place shallots and white wine in a saucepan and reduce by 90%.

- In a small saucepan, heat butter.

- A few minutes before serving, pour reduction into upright electric mixer. Add salt, pepper, and incorporate hot butter while machine is running. At the last moment, add lemon juice.

- Serve goatfish in leaf wrap; when opened they emit a wonderful aroma. The lemon butter enhances their flavor.

- 4 tilefish 240 g (1 lb)
- 24 pickled grape leaves
- Salt and fresh ground pepper
- 125 g (1 ¼ cups) skinned pistachios, chopped or ground
- 60 ml (¼ cup) cooking oil
- 20 g (1 cup) powdered mushrooms
- 60 g (⅓ cup) shallots, finely chopped
- 175 ml (¾ cup) white wine
- 240 g (1 lb) unsalted butter, clarified
- Salt and fresh ground white pepper
- 1 lemon, juiced

ALTERNATIVE FISH CHOICES

Sea robin, red gurnard, redfish, sea bream, scorpion fish, bluefish, samson fish, sheepshead, red snapper.

Sweet and Sour John Dory
with Fig and Grapefruit Sauce

4 servings · Difficulty: 4 · Preparation: 20 min · Cooking time: 10 min

- 4 Prickly pears[1]
- Juice of 2 grapefruits
- 75 g (⅓ cup) sugar
- 250 ml (1 cup) fish stock (see recipe pg. 12)
- White roux (see recipe pg. 12)
- 60 g (¼ cup) unsalted butter
- 60 g (⅓ cup) shallots, finely chopped
- 4 John Dory filets 120 g to 150 g (4 oz to 5 oz) each
- 125 ml (½ cup) white wine
- 30 g (1 cup) flat leaf parsley, scissor cut

ALTERNATIVE FISH CHOICES

Seabream, porgy, gurnard, redfish, sea robin.

SAUCE AIGRE-DOUCE

- Extract juice of figs without crushing seeds. Add grapefruit juice and sugar. In a saucepan, cook until mixture caramelizes at 165°C (330°F).

- Slowly add 125 ml (½ cup) fish stock. Reduce heat and thicken with a little white roux until desired consistency. Taste and season. Keep hot.

- Preheat oven to 85°C (175°F).

- Butter an oven-proof baking dish. Add shallots and top with fish filets. Pour on white wine and remaining fish stock. Cover with parchment paper or aluminum foil and bake to 68°C (155°F) at the thickest part.

- At the end of cooking, add cooking juices to the sauce.

- Coat bottom of heated plates with sauce. Top with filet and garnish with parsley.

- Serve with rice.

INFORMATION

(1) **Prickly pear:** Fruit of cactus opuntia. The granular structure of the pulp is composed of infinite small seeds. Tequila is produced from this cactus fruit.

Bream with Sea Urchin Cream

4 servings · Difficulty: 6 · Preparation: 40 min · Cooking time: 30 min

- Bone bream from inside, keeping the head. Salt, pepper, and refrigerate.

- Hold sea urchins with a potholder and open by cutting with scissors. Separate roe from juice, using a strainer. Place roe in a container lined with absorbent paper, cover with plastic wrap, and refrigerate. Reserve juice.

- Dilute sea urchin juice with 125 ml (½ cup) white Noilly-Prat vermouth and put through fine mesh strainer. Set aside.

- In a skillet, heat 60 g (¼ cup) of butter and gently cook carrot, celery, and leek. Salt and pepper, and pour sea urchin juice mixture over mixture. Cook on low until all liquid has evaporated. Adjust seasonings and cool.

- Open sea bream and stuff with vegetable mixture. Close. Salt and pepper.

- Preheat oven to 200°C (400°F).

- Generously brush oven-proof baking dish with remaining butter and place bream in bottom. Pour the remaining sea urchin juice and white vermouth over fish and cover with parchment paper or aluminum foil. Bake 20 to 30 minutes according to thickness of fish until they reach 68°C (155°F) at thickest part.

- Meanwhile, in a food processor, mix the sea urchin roe, heated cream, and lemon juice.

- When sea bream is cooked, remove from baking dish and quickly remove the skin from both sides. Immediately stir cooking juices into sea urchin cream. Adjust seasonings.

INGREDIENTS

- 2 bream, preferably pink, 1 kg to 1.2 kg (2 lbs to 2 ½ lbs)
- Salt and fresh ground pepper
- 8 sea urchins
- 310 ml (1 ¼ cups) white Noilly-Prat vermouth
- 180 g (¾ cup) unsalted butter
- ½ carrot, finely sliced lengthwise
- 1 celery stalk, finely sliced lengthwise
- ½ leek, white part, finely sliced lengthwise
- 250 ml (1 cup) fish stock (see recipe pg. 12)
- 175 ml (¾ cup) 35% cream
- Juice of 1 lemon
- 600 g (6 cups) small spring vegetables, as accompaniment

ALTERNATIVE FISH CHOICES

Redfish, red snapper, goatfish, searobin, poor cod, porgy, bass.

SERVING SUGGESTION

Place hot bream on heated plates and nappe (cover) with sauce. Serve immediately with streamed small spring vegetables.

Pan Fried Red Snapper, Chanterelle Mushrooms and Sea String Beans (Salicornia)

4 servings · Difficulty: 4 · Preparation: 15 min · Cooking time: 10 min

INGREDIENTS

- 300 g (10 oz) sea string beans (salicornia)
- 160 g (²/₃ cup) unsalted butter
- 300 g (5 cups) washed chanterelle mushrooms, drained and patted dry
- Salt and fresh ground pepper
- 45 g (¼ cup) shallots, chopped very fine
- 60 g (2 cups) parsley, chopped very fine
- Sifted flour
- 4 red snapper filets 150 g to 180 g (5 oz to 6 oz) each
- 60 ml (¼ cup) peanut or other cooking oil
- 175 ml (³/₄ cup) homemade thickened veal stock (see recipe pg. 17) or use store bought

PREPARATION

- In a saucepan of boiling water, blanch the sea beans several times to remove salt. Cool in cold water, drain and set aside.

- In a heavy-bottomed pan, heat 80 g (⅓ cup) butter and sauté chanterelles. Salt, pepper, and add shallots and parsley. Set aside.

- Flour snapper filets. Salt and pepper.

- In heavy-bottomed pan, heat remaining butter and oil and quickly sear filets on each side until golden. Reduce heat and cook until 68°C (155°F) at thickest part.

- Remove the filets and keep hot. In the cooking oil, quickly sauté sea beans until they are no longer watery.

ALTERNATIVE FISH CHOICES

Filets of sea bream, plaice, cod, pollock, goatfish, gurnard, tuna, shark, red grouper, mahi-mahi, albacore tuna.

SERVING SUGGESTION

Place vegetables (chanterelles and sea beans) on a hot plate, top with red snapper, and pour hot veal stock around filet.

Monkfish Medallions in Red Wine

4 servings · Difficulty: 2 · Preparation: 40 min · Cooking time: 15 min

Monkfish, or eelpout, is an ideal choice to introduce children to eating fish, since it has very few bones and a mild flavor.

• Pour red wine in saucepan; add shallots and reduce by 90%. Add fish stock, simmer several minutes, and thicken with white roux. Salt, pepper, and set aside.

• In a skillet, sauté mushrooms until all liquid has evaporated. Salt, pepper, and keep warm.

• In a saucepan of boiling water, cook small onions. Drain.

• Blanch salt pork, run under water and drain.

• Into a thick-bottomed pan, pour oil and fry salt pork until slightly golden. Add small onions and mushrooms.

• Place a steamer in a frying pan with 2 cm (¾") water in the bottom. Salt and pepper the monkfish medallions and steam until they reach 68°C (155°F) at the thickest part.

• Meanwhile, mix the sauce and vegetables together and reheat.

• As soon as the medallions are cooked, place on hot plates and nappe (cover) with red wine sauce.

• Boiled potatoes or rice are an excellent carbohydrate food to accompany this dish. Garlic-rubbed croûtons may also be served.

INGREDIENTS

• 310 ml (1 ¼ cups) robust red wine
• 90 g (½ cup) shallots, finely chopped
• 310 ml (1 ¼ cups) fish stock (see recipe pg. 12)
• White roux (see recipe pg. 12)
• Salt and fresh ground pepper
• 300 g (5 cups) white mushrooms, washed and diced
• 240 g (1 lb) pearl onions, peeled
• 210 g (7 oz) salt pork, diced
• 30 ml (2 tbsp) cooking onion
• 16 monkfish (or eelpout) medallions 40 g (1 ½ oz) each
• 300 g (2 ½ cups) potatoes or rice, cooked, as accompaniment

---

ALTERNATIVE FISH CHOICES

Shark, grouper, tuna, mahi-mahi.

Steamed Tilapia with Mushroom Clam Spread

INGREDIENTS

- 60 g (¼ cup) unsalted butter
- 400 g (6 ½ cups) firm white mushrooms, washed and chopped
- 250 ml (1 cup) clam juice
- Salt and fresh ground pepper
- 4 tilapia filets 180 g (6 oz) each
- 80 g (⅓ cup) soft butter (room temperature)
- 120 g (4 oz) chopped clams
- 20 g (⅔ cup) parsley, chopped

PREPARATION

MUSHROOM CLAM SPREAD

- In a skillet, heat butter and cook mushrooms until liquid is evaporated. Salt, pepper, and add 60 ml (¼ cup) clam juice. Keep hot.

TILAPIA

- In a large steamer, bring remaining clam juice to the boil.
- Season tilapia filets and steam for 3 to 6 minutes. Keep hot.
- Pour cooking juices from tilapia in bowl of a standing electric mixer. Add soft butter, cream and stir in clams and parsley to complete the sauce.

> **SERVING SUGGESTION**
>
> On each plate, make a base of mushroom, spread and top with tilapia filet. Nappe (cover) with clam sauce.

Redfish with Whole Grain Mustard

- 4 redfish filets 150 g (5 oz) each
- 310 ml (1 ¼ cups) 35% cream
- Salt and fresh ground pepper
- 80 ml (⅓ cup) olive oil
- 105 ml (7 tbsp) whole grain Meaux or Dijon mustard
- 160 ml (⅔ cup) thickened veal stock, fresh or canned (see recipe pg. 17)
- 7 g (¼ cup) tarragon, finely chopped

- Wipe redfish well and refrigerate.
- In a saucepan, reduce cream to half and set aside.
- Salt and pepper the redfish filets. Heat oil in a heavy-bottomed skillet and sear filets until slightly crusted on each side. Reduce heat and brush redfish filets with 75 ml (5 tbsp) Meaux or Dijon mustard. Place filets in heated oven.
- Add veal stock, remaining mustard, and tarragon to reduced cream. Salt and pepper to taste.

> **SERVING SUGGESTION**
>
> Pour mustard sauce in bottom of each plate and top with redfish filet. Serve with small steamed potatoes.

> **ALTERNATIVE FISH CHOICES**
>
> Grouper, tilefish, monkfish, swordfish, mahi-mahi, spiny dogfish.

Searobin or Gurnard Filets
with Diced Vegetables and Seaweed

4 servings · Difficulty: 3 · Preparation: 25 min · Cooking time: 30 min

- In a skillet, heat butter; add shallots, finely diced vegetables, and lemon, and braise for 1 to 2 minutes. Taste and adjust seasonings.

- Add Noilly-Prat vermouth, Campari, fish stock, and bouquet garni. Salt and pepper, and cook for 6 to 8 minutes. Taste and adjust seasonings.

- Preheat oven to 250°C (480°F).

- Wipe filets well; salt and pepper interior and exterior of filets.

- In an oven-proof baking dish, arrange fish alternating head to tail and pour fish stock sauce over fish, making sure that it also coats bottom of baking dish. Add dried seaweed.

- Cover with parchment paper or aluminum foil. Bake until 68°C (155°F) at thickest part (5 to 8 minutes).

- Serve very hot with cooking juices, accompanied with small potatoes cooked in salted boiling water, and garnished with parsley.

- 80 g (⅓ cup) unsalted butter
- 60 g (⅓ cup) shallots, finely chopped
- 150 g (2 ½ cups) firm white mushrooms, finely diced
- 50 g (½ cup) carrots, finely diced
- 1 stalk celery, finely diced
- ½ leek white, finely diced
- ½ yellow pepper, finely diced
- 2 parsley roots, finely diced
- Flesh of a peeled lemon, finely diced
- 125 ml (½ cup) Noilly-Prat vermouth, or white wine
- 60 ml (¼ cup) Suze or Campari (optional)
- 175 ml (¾ cup) fish stock (see recipe pg. 12)
- 1 bouquet garni
- Salt and fresh ground pepper
- 8 searobin filets 80 g to 130 g (2 ½ oz to 4 ½ oz) each
- 5 g (¼ cup) dried seaweed, chopped
- 400 g (¾ lb) small potatoes
- 20 g (⅔ cup) parsley, finely chopped

ALTERNATIVE FISH CHOICES

Goatfish, amberjack, porgy, gurnard, robinfish, sea bream.

INFORMATION

The gurnard fish family is rare in the North Atlantic; however, the searobin is available but not well known or often prepared in North American cuisine.

INGREDIENTS

- 800 g (8 cups) celery root, large cube
- 500 g (2 cups) potatoes, large cube
- 625 ml (2 ½ cups) milk
- Salt to taste
- ½ bay leaf
- 1 sprig thyme
- 160 g (1 ¼ cups) pine nuts
- 80 g (⅓ cup) unsalted butter
- 80 ml (⅓ cup) cooking oil
- Sifted flour
- 4 wolffish filets 180 g (6 oz) each
- Salt and fresh ground pepper
- 125 ml (½ cup) hot homemade thickened veal stock (see recipe pg. 17) or commercially prepared
- 20 g (⅔ cup) chervil leaves

PREPARATION

- In a saucepan, put celery root, potatoes, milk, salt, bay leaf, and thyme. Bring to a boil and then simmer until vegetables are tender.

- Meanwhile, in a heavy-bottomed skillet, toast the pine nuts, moving pan continuously, until pine nuts are golden.

- When cooked, drain vegetables well, put through a potato ricer or food mill, thin out with cooking juices, and add butter. Incorporate pine nuts and keep hot.

- In a heavy-bottomed skillet, heat butter and oil. Flour each wolffish filet and sear each side. Reduce heat and cook until fish is 68°C (155°F) at thickest part. Salt and pepper.

- On each plate, form a base of celery purée and pine nuts and top with filet. Surround each purée base with thickened veal stock and chervil leaves.

ALTERNATIVE FISH CHOICES

Lingcod, red grouper, cod, saithe, pollock, whiting.

NOTE:

It is important not to confuse American bass with European bass, also called wolffish. European bass is not well known or often prepared here, but is of high quality.

INFORMATION

Why potatoes with celery root? The celery root gives body to the otherwise too soft potato purée.

OTHER ASSORTED FAMILIES

In this fish group are the smallest (American smelt) as well as the largest (shark). For food consumption, the shark family has nine sub-families which are differentiated by their tail, dorsal fin, and even their gills. Alone in its family, the swordfish (*xiphioides*) is highly prized as a culinary delicacy. Merlin and white merlin belong to the *istiophoridae* family. The American conger eel (*congridae*), spiny dogfish (*squalidae*), mahi-mahi (*coryphaenidae*), ocean pout (*zoarcidae*), and blue runner (*carangidae*) deserve to be better known from a culinary standpoint. These fish can live in coastal or deep waters. Each of them, when cooked, will have its own distinctive flavor.

Other Assorted Families

 Small    Medium    Large

Maximum ★★★★; $$$$$
"Commonly Called" includes nicknames and misnomers

Swordfish

Scientific name: *Xiphias gladius* (Linné, 1758). **Commonly called:** Saber fish. **Characteristics:** Swordfish usually swim near the surface in waters at least 15°C (60°F). The back of the swordfish has purple metallic tones and blackish underbelly. It can grow to a very large size. **Quality:** ★★★★. **Cost:** $$$$.

Mahi-Mahi

Scientific name: *Coryphaena hippurus* (Linné, 1758). **Commonly called:** Sea bream, common mahi-mahi. **Characteristics:** Its average length is 1 m (40") but it can attain 2 m (6.5'). Its back is a metallic blue-green. **Quality:** ★★★. **Cost:** $$$.

Blue Shark/Blue Dog

Scientific name: *Prionace glauca* (Linné, 1758). **Commonly called:** Blueskin, squale. **Characteristics:** Its back is white, its nose long, its pectorals are long and sharp, and it can reach 3.80 m (12'). **Quality:** ★★★. **Cost:** $$$.

Mako/Shortfin Mako

Scientific name: *Isurus oxyrhinchus* (Rafinesque, 1810). **Commonly called:** Blue mako, shark mako. **Characteristics:** Its back is blue or dark greyish blue and its belly is white. It lives in rather warm and tropical waters. Size varies from 3 m to 3.70 m (10' to 12'), and can reach 4 m (13'). **Quality:** ★★★. **Cost:** $$$.

Spiny Dogfish

Scientific name: *Squalus acanthias* (Linné, 1758). **Commonly called:** Dogfish, sea dogfish, salmonette. **Characteristics:** Its back is dark grey, sometimes with brown added, and the belly varies from pale grey to white. This fish can measure up to 1.35 m (53") and can weigh up to 9.2 kg (20 lbs). **Quality:** ★★. **Cost:** $$.

Spotted Dogfish/Rock Salmon

Scientific name: *Scyliorhinus canicula, Scyliorhinus stellaris* (Linné, 1758). **Commonly called:** Dogfish, salmonette. **Characteristics:** These two fish are different in size: the spotted dogfish never goes beyond 80 cm (32"), and the rock salmon can reach 1.20 m (48"). Its yellow body is covered with many black markings. **Quality:** ★★. **Cost:** $$.

White Marlin/Marlin

Scientific name: *Tetrapturus pfluegeri* (Robins & de Sylva, 1963), *Istiophorus albicans* (Latreille, 1804). **Commonly called:** Marlin. **Characteristics:** These two cousins from the Istiophoridae family are often of the same size—2.50 m to 3 m (8' to 10'). Their back is about the same color (blue-black or dark blue). The flanks are silver. **Quality:** ★★★★. **Cost:** $$$$.

American Conger Eel

Scientific name: *Conger oceanicus* (Mitchill, 1818). **Commonly called:** Sea serpent. **Characteristics:** The American conger eel can reach 2.10 m (7') and 10 kg (22 lbs). Color is generally grey and its belly is white. **Quality:** ★★★. **Cost:** $$.

Ocean Pout

Scientific name: *Macrozoarces americanus* (Bloch & Schneider, 1801). **Commonly called:** Eelpout. **Characteristics:** Its color varies from yellowish to reddish brown, sprinkled with grey or olive green markings. It can reach 1.15 m (3' 8") and a weight of 5.5 kg (12 lbs), but most are 80 cm (31½") long. **Quality:** ★★★. **Cost:** $$$.

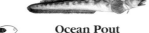

Blue Runner/Marlin

Scientific name: *Caranx crysos* (Mitchill, 1815). **Commonly called:** Hard tail, yellow jack. **Characteristics:** The back is green. The lower parts of the flanks and belly are silvery or golden. This fish can reach a length of 60 cm (24") and a weight of 1.8 kg (4 lbs). **Quality:** ★★★. **Cost:** $$.

American Smelt

Scientific name: *Osmerus mordax* (Mitchill, 1815). **Commonly called:** Smelt, rainbow smelt. **Characteristics:** The back has green tones with lighter green flanks with silver stripes and a silver belly. The whole body is sprinkled with small black dots. Length varies from 13 cm to 20 cm (5" to 8"). **Quality:** ★★★. **Cost:** $$.

Grilled Swordfish
with Caper Compote

4 servings · Difficulty: 3 · Preparation: 20 min · Cooking time: 15 min

PREPARATION

INGREDIENTS

- In a skillet, heat butter and sauté mushrooms until liquid has evaporated. Salt and pepper. Set aside.

- In a bowl, mix fresh herbs, capers, and mushrooms, making a compote. Set aside.

- Wipe swordfish steaks well, salt, pepper, and brush well with oil.

- Heat the grill using three heats (see pg. 27). Grill, turning steaks to form square grill marks on each side. Reduce heat and cook until 68°C (155°F) is reached at thickest part.

- Meanwhile, in a blender or bowl of a food processor, blend oyster juice, olive oil, and lemon juice until an emulsion is formed. Stir in the compote gently and adjust seasonings.

- 80 g (⅓ cup) unsalted butter
- 300 g (5 cups) firm white mushrooms, washed and chopped
- Salt and pepper
- 25 g (¾ cup) tarragon, chopped
- 40 g (1 cup) parsley, stalks removed, and chopped
- 15 g (½ cup) fresh thyme, chopped
- 60 g (¼ cup) capers, chopped
- 4 swordfish steaks 180 g (6 oz) each
- Salt and pepper
- 60 ml (¼ cup) cooking oil
- 125 ml (½ cup) oyster juice
- 125 ml (½ cup) olive oil
- Juice of 1 lemon

ALTERNATIVE FISH CHOICES

Mahi-mahi, white marlin, mako, spiney dogfish, marlin, monk fish, salmon, cod, haddock.

SERVING SUGGESTIONS

Place swordfish steaks on heated plates and top with compote. Serve extra compote in gravy boat. Small sautéed potatoes are a good accompaniment.

Mahi-mahi
with Grapefruit and Campari

- 4 mahi-mahi slices 180 g (6 oz) each
- Salt and pepper
- Sifted flour
- 60 g (¼ cup) unsalted butter
- 60 ml (¼ cup) cooking oil
- 160 ml (⅔ cup) sunflower oil
- 160 ml (⅔ cup) grapefruit sections (membranes removed)
- 160 ml (⅔ cup) Campari[1]
- Salt and pepper

ALTERNATIVE FISH CHOICES

Swordfish, white marlin, mako, spiny dogfish, marlin, monk fish, salmon, cod, haddock.

SERVING SUGGESTIONS

Place mahi-mahi slices on very hot plates, accompanied with mashed potatoes or small bite-sized potatoes boiled in salted water. The mix of Campari, grapefruit, and oil complements the texture of mahi-mahi.

- Wipe mahi-mahi slices well. Salt, pepper, and flour.

- In a thick-bottomed skillet, heat butter and oil. Sear mahi-mahi on both sides until golden, reduce heat, and cook until 68°C (155°F) is reached at thickest part.

- Meanwhile, heat oil to 70°C (160°F), and sauté grapefruit sections. Stir gently with a whisk until the pulp breaks up. Add Campari and seasonings.

INFORMATION

(1) **Campari**: Italian aperitif, refreshing, with a bitter taste, as is Suze or gentiane alcohol.

Breaded Blue Shark
with Shallot Butter

4 servings · Difficulty: 3 · Preparation: 20 min
· Cooking time: by thermometer

FRESH BREAD CRUMBS

• Remove crusts of sliced bread and chop bread slices in food processor. Refrigerate in airtight container. It will keep for one month.

COATING PROCESS

1. A cooking sheet with sifted flour.

2. Beaten egg and milk mixture.

3. A cooking sheet with bread crumbs.

• In a small saucepan, heat 60 g (¼ cup) butter and sweat shallots. Add Noilly-Prat vermouth and cook 5 more minutes. Add 2 pinches sea salt and cool.

• Incorporate remaining butter, lemon juice, pepper, and correct seasoning if necessary. Keep at room temperature.

BLUE SHARK

• Preheat oven to 150°C (300°F).

• Wipe each piece of shark well, salt and pepper, and divide saffron between each fish piece.

• Flour each shark piece. Dip in beaten egg and milk mixture, and coat with fresh breadcrumbs.

• In a heavy-bottomed skillet, heat shallot butter and add shark pieces. (They will quickly absorb the butter, which is normal).

• Sauté each piece on both sides until golden, and continue cooking until 68°C (155°F) is reached at thickest part.

FRESH BREAD CRUMBS
• 1 loaf sliced white bread

COATING PROCESS
• 100 g (²/₃ cup) sifted flour
• 1 egg
• 125 ml (½ cup) milk

BLUE SHARK
• 4 thick pieces shark 180 g (6 oz) each
• 1 pinch saffron stamens or saffron threads, chopped
• Salt and fresh ground pepper
• 160 g (²/₃ cup) lemon shallot butter

SHALLOT LEMON BUTTER
• 300 g (1 ¼ cup) unsalted butter (room temperature)
• 90 g (½ cup) shallots, finely chopped
• 125 ml (½ cup) Noilly-Prat vermouth
• Sea salt
• Juice of 1 lemon
• Fresh ground white pepper

ALTERNATIVE FISH CHOICES

Swordfish, monk fish, mahi-mahi, tunny fish, tuna, yellowfin tuna, tilefish, marlin, white marlin.

SERVING SUGGESTION

Serve as soon as bread crumb coating is crusty. Small seasonal vegetables are a good accompaniment.

Country Style Roasted Marlin

INGREDIENTS

- 1 marlin roast, no skin 1.2 g to 1.5 kg (2 ½ lbs to 3 lbs)
- Salt and fresh ground pepper
- 1 thin piece of fresh pork fat to wrap roast, or fatty bacon
- 80 ml (⅓ cup) olive oil
- 150 g (1 cup) small white or red onions
- 150 g (5 oz) smoked salt fat back, diced 0.5 cm x 2 cm (¼" x ¾")
- 250 g (2 ½ cups) firm white mushrooms, quartered
- 250 ml (1 cup) veal stock (see recipe pg. 17)
- 300 g (2 ½ cups) potato balls made with small melon scoop
- 30 g (1 cup) parsley, chopped

ALTERNATIVE FISH CHOICES

Shark, white marlin, swordfish, mahi-mahi, tunny fish, tuna, yellowfin tuna.

SERVING SUGGESTIONS

Cut thick slices of marlin, nappe (cover) with cooking juices and surround with vegetables. Garnish with parsley.

PREPARATION

- Preheat oven to 170°C (340°F).

- Salt and pepper marlin. Wrap well with fatty bacon or pork fat large enough to wrap fish, and tie well with string.

- In a high-sided cooking pot or casserole, heat oil and sear fish roast well on all sides. Add small onions and salt fat, and bake, covered, in the oven. Baste frequently. As soon as 50°C (120°F) is reached in center of roast, drain cooking fat, add mushrooms and veal stock. Continue cooking, basting frequently, until 68°C (155°F) is reached in center of roast.

- Remove roast and cook noisette potatoes (potato balls formed with a small melon scoop) in cooking juices. Adjust seasonings.

Conger Eel à la Catalane

4 servings · Difficulty: 4 · Preparation: 40 min · Cooking time: 20 to 30 min

CATALANE

- Remove stems of 8 tomatoes, skin, seed, and cut into small dice.

- Heat oil, and sear onions and garlic. Add tomatoes, thyme, parsley, rosemary, bay leaf, and olives. Salt and pepper, and simmer 20 to 30 minutes until all liquid is evaporated.

EEL

- Preheat oven to 90°C (190°F).

- Salt and pepper eel slices, and place in an oven-proof baking dish large enough for the eel to be completely covered with the catalane.

- Drizzle a little olive oil on top and cover with parchment paper. Bake until 68°C (155°F) is reached at the thickest part. Cooking at a low temperature keeps the fish flesh tender and moist.

- Serve immediately, accompanied with potatoes mousseline (puréed).

CATALANE

- 8 ripe tomatoes (in season) or 2 cans Italian tomatoes
- 60 ml (¼ cup) olive oil
- 1 Spanish onion 120 g (4 oz), finely diced
- 3 cloves garlic, chopped
- 1 fresh sprig thyme, finely chopped
- 30 g (1 cup) parsley leaves, finely chopped
- 2 rosemary sprigs, finely chopped
- 1 bay leaf
- 210 g (1 ¾ cups) pitted black olives
- Salt and fresh ground pepper

EEL

- 4 slices conger eel 180 g to 210 g (6 oz to 7 oz) each

ALTERNATIVE FISH CHOICES

Tunny fish, mako shark, yellowfin tuna, swordfish, white marlin, tuna, monk fish.

INGREDIENTS

- 8 ocean pout filets 90 g to 120 g (3 oz to 4 oz) each
- Salt and pepper
- 175 ml (¾ cup) dry white wine
- 90 g (½ cup) shallots, finely chopped
- 800 g (28 oz) small mussels
- Veloutine or corn starch, rice or potatoes, as a thickener
- 250 ml (1 cup) 35% cream
- Juice of 1 lime
- 25 g (½ cup) chives, scissor cut, or chopped parsley

ALTERNATIVE FISH CHOICES

Filets of sole, plaice, flet, lemon sole or slippery flounder, summer flounder.

SERVING SUGGESTION

Serve hot with very small potatoes (Parisienne potatoes) cooked in salted water, and garnished with chives or chopped parsley.

Rolled Ocean Pout Filets with Mussels

PREPARATION

- Flatten ocean pout filets as shown below. Salt and pepper and set aside.

TECHNIQUE FOR FLATTENING FISH:

Place filets between two sheets of aluminum foil.

Tap gently

Flatten filet.

- In a casserole, add white wine, shallots, and mussels, and cook, covered, until mussels open. Remove from heat immediately. Let cool and remove mussels from shell. Place two mussels in center of each filet and roll.

- Preheat oven to 150°C (300 F).

- Place filet rolls in oven-proof baking dish and pour mussel cooking juices over filets. Cover with parchment paper and bake until small white, pearl-like drops appear on filet. Remove fish rolls and place on paper towelling and keep hot. In a small saucepan, reduce cream by half and add lime juice.

- Using veloutine, thicken the cooking juices, add the cream, and adjust seasonings.

- Return the rolls to the thickened sauce and add remaining mussels.

Beignet Smelt Fritters

4 servings · Difficulty: 2 · Preparation: 30 min · Cooking time: 5 min

BEIGMET BATTER

- Put flour in a bowl and make a well in the center.

- Separate egg yolks from the whites. Pour yolks in well along with salt, pepper, and 125 ml (½ cup) beer. Leave a few minutes to allow the salt to dissolve. While stirring, add remaining beer. Pour through a sieve and refrigerate at least 1 hour.

SMELTS

- Thirty minutes before beginning recipe preparations, wipe smelts well, salt, pepper, and leave at room temperature.

- Beat egg whites until firm and incorporate into fritter batter.

- Heat frying oil until very hot.

- Dip smelts in fritter batter and cook one by one, turning gently (1 to 2 minutes will suffice to cook, forming a crispy exterior). Serve immediately with lemon quarters.

BEIGNET BATTER

- 500 g (3 ⅓ cups) sifted flour
- 4 eggs
- Salt and ground white pepper
- 375 ml (1 ½ cups) pale beer

SMELTS

- 600 g (20 oz) smelts, preferably small
- Egg whites (see above)
- Frying oil
- 1 lemon, quartered

ALTERNATIVE FISH CHOICES

Small perch, small poor cod, small anchovies.

---

124   OTHER ASSORTED FAMILIES

FRESH WATER FISH

There are 24 families and 137 species of fish in Canada, 181 if we include the exotic species that were imported and survived. We have already devoted a chapter to the salmonids, a high quality fish that is plentiful. Other noteworthy freshwater fish are covered in this chapter. Two fish are particular favorites: pickerel and perch. In early spring, perch filets have a wonderful flavor, while in summer, pickerel keeps anglers happy. But what about Atlantic sturgeon? This fish has existed since the late-cretaceous age. Sturgeon can live from 50 to 80 years, depending on the sex. This magnificent fish is mostly eaten smoked, but sturgeon caviar from Russia or Iran is also popular. In the seventeenth and eighteenth centuries, sturgeon was served primarily to the aristocracy.

Fresh Water Fish

Small Medium Large

Maximum ★★★★; $$$$$
"Commonly Called" includes nicknames and misnomers

Yellow Perch

Scientific name: *Perca flavescens* (Mitchill, 1814). **Commonly called:** Perch. **Characteristics:** This fish is highly prized by cooks. In early spring its body is green and golden brown and has seven stripes of decreasing width on the belly. Its average length is 20 cm (8") and its average weight about 100 g (3 oz). **Quality:** ★★★. **Cost:** $$.

Pickerel

Scientific name: *Stizostedion vitreum* (Mitchill, 1818). **Commonly called:** Walleye, White pickerel. **Characteristics:** Perch and pickerel are cousins. This fish, with lean and white flesh, has brown and yellow tones with a white belly. Its weight can reach 4.5 kg to 5.5 kg (10 lbs to 12 lbs). **Other pickerel:** Sand pickerel – *Stizostedion canadense*; Pikeperch – *Lucio perca*. **Quality:** ★★★★. **Cost:** $$$.

Northern Pike

Scientific name: *Esox lucius* (Linné, 1758), *Esox niger* (Lesueur, 1818). **Commonly called:** Chain Pickerel, Lake Pickerel. **Characteristics:** This fish can reach a very great length and weight. Its flesh is in the green and brown tones, and its body is sprinkled with pale markings. Even though it has a lot of bones, it's a wonderful culinary experience. **Same family:** Tiger muskellunge – *Esox masquinongy*; Chain pickerel – *Esox niger*; Redfin pickerel – *Esox americanus*; Grass pickerel – *Esox vermiculatus*. **Quality:** ★★★. **Cost:** $$.

American Eel/Common Eel

Scientific name: *Anguilla rostrata* (Lesueur, 1817). **Commonly called:** Common eel. **Characteristics:** Its meat is fatty and dark. Its back is in the black and brown tones, its flanks are yellow, and its belly is a yellowish white. Average length is from 70 cm to 100 cm (27" to 39") and average weight from 1.1 kg to 1.6 kg (2½ lbs to 3½ lbs). **Quality:** ★★★. **Cost:** $$.

Smallmouth Bass

Scientific name: *Micropterus dolomieu* (Lacepède, 1802). **Commonly called:** Largemouth bass. **Characteristics:** Its flesh is white and flaky. Its back is in the green and brown tones with small golden marks. The belly is cream to off-white. Average length is 20 cm to 38 cm (8" to 15") and weight from 240 g to 560 g (8 oz to 20 oz). **Quality:** ★★★. **Cost:** $$.

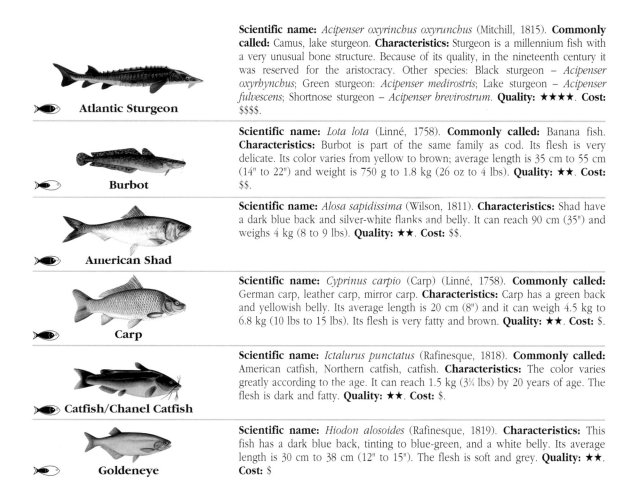

Scientific name: *Acipenser oxyrinchus oxyrunchus* (Mitchill, 1815). **Commonly called:** Camus, lake sturgeon. **Characteristics:** Sturgeon is a millennium fish with a very unusual bone structure. Because of its quality, in the nineteenth century it was reserved for the aristocracy. Other species: Black sturgeon – *Acipenser oxyrhynchus*; Green sturgeon: *Acipenser medirostris*; Lake sturgeon – *Acipenser fulvescens*; Shortnose sturgeon – *Acipenser brevirostrum*. **Quality:** ★★★★. **Cost:** $$$$.

Atlantic Sturgeon

Scientific name: *Lota lota* (Linné, 1758). **Commonly called:** Banana fish. **Characteristics:** Burbot is part of the same family as cod. Its flesh is very delicate. Its color varies from yellow to brown; average length is 35 cm to 55 cm (14" to 22") and weight is 750 g to 1.8 kg (26 oz to 4 lbs). **Quality:** ★★. **Cost:** $$.

Burbot

Scientific name: *Alosa sapidissima* (Wilson, 1811). **Characteristics:** Shad have a dark blue back and silver-white flanks and belly. It can reach 90 cm (35") and weighs 4 kg (8 to 9 lbs). **Quality:** ★★. **Cost:** $$.

American Shad

Scientific name: *Cyprinus carpio* (Carp) (Linné, 1758). **Commonly called:** German carp, leather carp, mirror carp. **Characteristics:** Carp has a green back and yellowish belly. Its average length is 20 cm (8") and it can weigh 4.5 kg to 6.8 kg (10 lbs to 15 lbs). Its flesh is very fatty and brown. **Quality:** ★★. **Cost:** $.

Carp

Scientific name: *Ictalurus punctatus* (Rafinesque, 1818). **Commonly called:** American catfish, Northern catfish, catfish. **Characteristics:** The color varies greatly according to the age. It can reach 1.5 kg (3¼ lbs) by 20 years of age. The flesh is dark and fatty. **Quality:** ★★. **Cost:** $.

Catfish/Chanel Catfish

Scientific name: *Hiodon alosoides* (Rafinesque, 1819). **Characteristics:** This fish has a dark blue back, tinting to blue-green, and a white belly. Its average length is 30 cm to 38 cm (12" to 15"). The flesh is soft and grey. **Quality:** ★★. **Cost:** $

Goldeneye

Yellow Perch Mousseline "Mère Jeanne"

4 servings · Difficulty: 3 · Preparation: 40 min · Cooking time: 20 min

This recipe was a great success in the French pavilion's restaurants during Expo '67 in Montreal. Perch has a reputation for being inedible—too bony, not very tasty, etc.—but is, in fact, an exceptionally fine culinary treat.

• Wash perch filets and put through a meat grinder twice (first time with medium setting, second time with fine setting, but do not grind in a food processor). To achieve the best results, place ground filet in door of freezer for 1 hour to chill until very cold but not frozen.

• Incorporate eggs one by one into the chilled flesh. Salt and pepper, add nutmeg, and stir in butter, 1 spoon at a time. This is the most difficult part of the recipe since raw fish doesn't blend easily with fat.

• As soon as the mixture is smooth, incorporate the very chilled cream, 1–2°C (33–34°F). The mixture should be very smooth.

• Using a "corne" (scraper)[1], press through a sieve, put in a pastry bag, and squeeze mixture generously into buttered molds.

• Place molds in pan with water not hotter than 90°C (190°F) halfway up sides and oven bake.

• When cooked, unmold on hot plates and nappe (cover) with lobster sauce (see recipe pg. 16).

• Rice pilaf is a good accompaniment.

Ingredients:
- 700 g (1 ½ lbs) fresh perch filets (do not use frozen perch)
- 3 eggs
- Salt and ground white pepper
- 1 pinch ground nutmeg
- 180 g (¾ cup) unsalted butter (room temperature)
- 175 ml (¾ cup) 35% cream
- 310 ml (1 ¼ cups) hollandaise sauce (see recipe pg. 13)
- 260 g (2 cups) rice pilaf, cooked

INFORMATION

(1) **Corne:** a utensil used to scrape dough or fondue mixture.

INGREDIENTS

- 1 eel 600 g to 800 g (21 oz to 28 oz)
- 60 g (¼ cup) unsalted butter
- 100 g (2 cups) sorrel leaves
- 25 g (½ cup) nettle leaves
- 20 g (½ cup) flat leaf parsley
- 5 ml (1 tsp) salad burnet[1]
- 5 ml (1 tsp) green sage
- 5 ml (1 tsp) savoury
- 2 ½ ml (½ tsp) tarragon
- 5 ml (1 tsp) chervil
- 1 pinch fresh thyme
- 500 ml (2 cups) blond beer
- Salt and fresh ground pepper
- Rice flour

ALTERNATIVE FISH CHOICES
Spiney dogfish, conger eel, spotted dogfish, or rock salmon.

PREPARATION

4 servings • Difficulty: 2 • Preparation: 20 min • Cooking time: 10 to 15 min

In North America, most eels are fished but very few are consumed. The Belgians, however, make a specialty of eel, which I am going to help you "discover."

- Cut eel into 5 cm (2") slices.

- In a skillet, heat butter, and add sorrel, nettle, parsley, salad burnet, green sage, savory, tarragon, and chervil. "Sweat" until they are limp. Add thyme. Tie the eel slices to hold their shape.

- Pour beer over all, and salt and pepper. Cook approximately 10 to 15 minutes, then thicken the juices with rice flour so that they are not too thin at the end of cooking. This recipe is usually eaten cold.

INFORMATION
(1) **Salad burnet** is a cucumber-flavored herb.

Roast Sturgeon and Mushrooms

4 servings · Difficulty: 3 · Preparation: 35 min
· Cooking time: by thermometer

The flesh of sturgeon is similar to white meat.

- Preheat oven to 200°C (400°F).

- Tie the sturgeon around its circumference in several places; salt and pepper. In a high-sided heavy skillet or casserole dish, heat butter and oil and cook sturgeon, turning gently and sautéing each side.

- Cover and oven bake, basting frequently.

- As soon as the roasted sturgeon reaches 50°C (120°F) at the center, sprinkle small diced vegetables on top and continue cooking until 65°C (150°F) is reached. Remove skillet from oven and transfer roast to another container to keep hot.

- Put mushrooms in cooking juices, add white wine, fish stock, and veal stock. Cook until the mushrooms are well done. Adjust seasonings.

- 1 thick section of sturgeon, 1.2 kg (2 ½ lbs)
- Salt and fresh ground pepper
- 80 g (⅓ cup) unsalted butter
- 80 ml (⅓ cup) sunflower oil
- 240 g (1 lb) mixed vegetables, small dice
- 420 g (14 oz) button mushrooms
- 160 ml (⅔ cup) dry white wine
- 160 ml (⅔ cup) fish stock (see recipe pg. 12)
- 160 ml (⅔ cup) thickened veal stock (see recipe pg. 17)

ALTERNATIVE FISH CHOICES

Shark, swordfish, tunny fish.

SERVING SUGGESTION

Remove string from sturgeon. Divide the cooking juices, mushrooms, and diced vegetables among heated plates. Top with a thick slice of roasted sturgeon. Mashed potatoes are a good accompaniment.

Smallmouth Bass Fritters
with Hollandaise Sauce

INGREDIENTS

- 500 g (3 ½ cups) sifted flour
- Salt and fresh ground pepper
- 3 egg yolks
- 310 ml (1 ¼ cups) dark beer
- 600 g (20 oz) smallmouth bass filets
- 4 egg whites
- 175 ml (¾ cup) hollandaise sauce
  (see recipe pg. 13)

PREPARATION

- To make batter, put flour in bowl, make a well in the center, add salt and pepper, pour in egg yolks, and incorporate beer by mixing all ingredients to form a firm batter. Refrigerate.

- Cut bass filets into 10 cm x 1.5 cm (4" x ½") strips and wrap in a clean tea towel.

- Beat egg whites and fold into chilled batter.

- Flour bass strips and dip 4 at a time in the batter. Fry in oil 250°C (480°F) until they are crisp on the outside and moist on the inside. Repeat procedure for remaining fish strips, keeping fritters hot in the front of the oven. Serve with hollandaise sauce.

SERVING SUGGESTIONS

Serve hollandaise sauce in small individual ramekins placed on plates.

Yellow Perch Filets in Almond Butter

- 120 g (1 cup) slivered almonds
- 180 g (¾ cup) unsalted butter
- Juice of 1 lemon
- Salt and fresh ground pepper
- 600 g (1 ⅓ lbs) yellow perch filets
- Oil for frying

- When preparing almond butter, it is important to leave butter out the night before to soften and come to room temperature.

- In a non-stick pan, toast almonds and then chop in a food processor.

- Gently mix the almonds, butter, lemon juice, salt, and pepper, and keep at room temperature.

- Wipe perch filets well, salt and pepper.

- Heat frying oil on high. Sear perch filets, 2 or 3 at a time, for 1 to 2 minutes. When seared, place them on a paper-towel-lined baking sheet and keep warm in the oven. Repeat this procedure for all perch filets.

ALTERNATIVE FISH CHOICES

Pickerel, smallmouth bass, lake whitefish, tilefish, cod, monk fish.

SERVING SUGGESTION

Place perch filets on very hot plates and nappe (cover) with almond butter.

Savory Shad Cakes Meunière
with Herbed Polenta

4 servings · Difficulty: 3 · Preparation: 30 min · Cooking time: 20 min

Shad have a flaky, high quality flesh. However, they have five small bones, which is why we prepare them as galettes (cakes).

- Put shad filets through meat grinder twice.

- Remove crusts from sliced bread and dip bread in cream then parsley. Add to ground shad and put mixture through grinder for third time.

- Rub through a sieve, and salt and pepper to taste.

- Form cakes 120g to 150 g (4 oz to 5 oz) each. Flour the cakes, then dip in egg yolk, milk, and almond mixture. Refrigerate.

- To prepare polenta, bring water to a boil; add oil. Using a whisk, gradually incorporate the corn flour while stirring constantly.

- Cook on very low heat for approximately 15 minutes, stirring from time to time. Salt and pepper to taste.

- In a heavy-bottomed pan, heat butter and lemon juice, and fry shad cakes gently in mixture. Don't use high heat or grilled almonds will burn.

INGREDIENTS

- 450 g (16 oz) shad filets
- 4 slices white bread
- 175 ml (³/₄ cup) 35% cream
- 25 g (³/₄ cup) parsley, stems removed
- Salt and fresh ground pepper
- Flour
- 2 beaten egg yolks
- 160 ml (²/₃ cup) milk
- 180 g (1 ¹/₂ cups) almonds, chopped and toasted
- 500 ml (2 cups) water
- 15 ml (1 tbsp) olive oil
- 125 g (³/₄ cup) corn flour
- Salt and fresh ground pepper
- 120 g (¹/₂ cup) unsalted butter
- Juice of 1 lemon
- 25 g (¹/₂ cup) chives, scissor cut
- 10 g (¹/₃ cup) chervil leaves

ALTERNATIVE FISH CHOICES

Pike, carp, lake whitefish.

SERVING SUGGESTION

Form serving-spoon shapes with polenta and place a few on each dinner plate. Top with shad cake and pour lemon butter over all. Garnish with chives and chervil.

Saffron Carrot Burbot Filets

- 2 carrots
- Salt and ground white pepper
- Juice of 2 fresh oranges
- Juice of 1 fresh grapefruit
- 160 ml (²/₃ cup) white wine
- 1 pinch saffron stamen[i]
- 4 burbot filets 180 g (6 oz) each
- Rice flour
- 240 g (8 oz) quinoa

ALTERNATIVE FISH CHOICES

Cod, Boston bluefish, haddock, pollock, cusk, ocean pout, whiting.

SERVING SUGGESTION

Place filets on heated plates, nappe (cover) with sauce, and accompany with cooked quinoa.

Along with the Atlantic tomcod, the burbot is the only fresh water fish in the same family as cod. It has a flaky flesh of excellent quality.

- Juice the carrots in a juicer. Salt and pepper. Put carrot juice in a bowl, mix in orange and grapefruit juices, white wine, saffron, and add the four burbot filets. Marinate at least 1 hour.

- In a casserole, poach burbot at a low temperature of 90°C (120°F) until they reach 68°C (155°F) at thickest part. Remove burbot and keep hot. Thicken cooking juices with rice flour. Adjust seasonings.

- While fish is cooking, cook quinoa in twice the amount of water (480 g/16 oz) for approximately 15 minutes.

INFORMATION

(1) **Saffron:** A seasoning made from the dried stamens of the saffron crocus. It may also be found in powdered form. It takes 28,000 crocuses to produce one kilogram of saffron.

Barbequed Herb Stuffed
Pickerel en Papillote

4 servings · Difficulty: 3 · Preparation: 25 min · Cooking time: 40 to 60 min

This recipe works well for the fisherman who wants to cook his catch over an open fire or on a barbecue. In winter it can be cooked in a fireplace.

• Keep the head and tail intact and scale the fish. Remove the bones through the stomach opening, being careful not to tear the flesh. Salt and pepper the inside and outside of the fish, wrap, and refrigerate.

• In a heavy-bottomed skillet, heat butter, add herbs, and cook until sizzling. Salt, pepper, and let cool.

• In a casserole, heat the white wine and fine diced vegetables, reducing by 90%. Then add fish stock. Salt, pepper, and let cool.

• Butter aluminum foil well, place herb-stuffed pickerel on top, and fold over to close, leaving a small opening on top.

• Pour cooking juices through opening, close as airtight as possible, and cook according to instructions for "grilled fish" (see method pg. 10). The same method can be for cooking in a fireplace.

- 1 pickerel 1.2 kg to 1.8 kg (2 ½ lbs to 4 lbs)
- Salt and fresh ground pepper
- 80 g (⅓ cup) unsalted butter
- 50 g (1 cup) sorrel, scissor cut
- 25 g (½ cup) chives, scissor cut
- 100 g (2 cups) spinach leaves, scissor cut
- 30 g (1 cup) celery leaves, scissor cut
- 25 g (¾ cup) parsley, scissor cut
- 20 g (½ cup) chervil, scissor cut
- Salt and fresh ground pepper
- 250 ml (1 cup) white wine
- 100 g (1 cup) vegetables, finely diced
- 175 ml (¾ cup) fish stock (see recipe pg. 12)
- 80 g (⅓ cup) unsalted butter
- 1 large sheet aluminum foil
- 4 potatoes

ALTERNATIVE FISH CHOICES

Sea bream, porgy, sea bass, striped bass, common whitefish, lake whitefish.

Index

Bibiography

W. B. Scott and A. H. Leim. *Poissons de la côte Atlantique du Canada, (Fish of Atlantic Canada)*. Office des Research Office, Department of Fisheries, Canada, Bulletin No. 155, 1972.

J. Gousset, G. Tixerant, M. Roblot, C. Holvoet and J. Jamet. *Les produits de la pêche. Informations techniques des services vétérinaires français, (Fish Products: Technical and Service Information for French Veterinarians)*. 2001.

Jean-Paul Grappe. *Poissons, mollusques et crustacés, (Fish, Mollusks, and Crustaceans)*. Montréal, Les Éditions de l'Homme, 1997.

Acknowledgements and Thanks

In the Madeleine Islands: Our thanks to the C.M.T.A. group and its operating director Monsieur Emmanuel Aucoin, who provided our transportation; La Marée Haute, Patrick Mathey and his team who received us so well; Carole and Ghislain of La Fouineuse Antiquaire; Johanne Vigneault of La Table des Roy; Berthe Vigneau of La Corporation des Acadiens; the hotel-restaurant La Petite Baie; Mrs. Linda Martinet; Josie and Louis, who lent us their residence, business, and accessories, and assisted us with photos; Dominique Gagnon and Brigitte Léger of Bon goût frais des îles; Ferland at d'Étang-du-Nord; Monsieur Willy Lebel (here, at left), fisheries representative and fishing expert. In Montreal: Mrs. Francine Larochelle and Mrs. Colette Villeneuve, for their fine work; Mr. Richard St-Pierre, of the fish store "La Mer" for supplying the fish. "Chez Louis" for supplying fruits and vegetables; Mr. Julien Bartolucci for his fish drawings.